AVIATION

The first seventy years

AVIATION
The first seventy years

Illustrations by John Young
Text by John Blake

ISBN 0 85674 020 9
Published by
Triune Books, London, England
© Trewin Copplestone Publishing Ltd 1973
Printed in England by
Ben Johnson & Co. Ltd., York

Introduction

The seventieth anniversary of the first controlled free
flight by a heavier-than-air machine seemed to be a very
good point in time to survey man's flying achievements.
Those three score years and ten have seen the birth of the
supersonic airliner (and a difficult and protracted birth
it has been) and the end of the first phase in the
exploration of space. The United States has completed
President Kennedy's Project Apollo and the Soviet Union
has ended its ten-year programme to establish an orbital
space station.
The United States, too, has its Skylab in orbit and in an
atmosphere (if the phrase is not incongruous) made rather
more favourable by the SALT agreement and the meeting of
the two heads of state, plans are being prepared for joint
space missions by the end of the decade.
This book is a contribution, in John Young's paintings and
drawings, to the commemoration of those hectic, sometimes
tragic, but significant years. The text that accompanies
them is planned to link the episodes of history and the
incidents and aircraft portrayed and to explain something
of the forces and circumstances and pressures – and the
ideas and the leaps in the dark – that gave rise to those
events and gave birth to those aircraft.
It is not as balanced or impartial a tale as we might
have liked it to be – it has turned out to be, for both of
us, a very personal selection from the great store of
aviation history. Inevitably, whole sections have been
cribbed and cabined or left out altogether, to do some
justice to what we have included. One has discovered, like
Horace, that: Brevis esse laboro, Obscurus fio,
"Whenever I struggle to be brief, I become
unintelligible."

John Blake

The toss of a coin gave Wilbur Wright the first chance of glory on 14th December, 1903, but he misjudged the sensitivity of the elevator and hit the sand as the **Flyer** rose from the take-off trolley. Orville's turn on 17th made him the first man to achieve properly authenticated flight.

The Men of Genius

Other experimenters preceded them and they drew inspiration from what had already been done, especially by Lilienthal in Germany and Chanute in America, but the story of controlled, practical flight in a powered aircraft begins with Wilbur and Orville Wright.

When they came to examine the technical writings then available, they discovered that most published data were very inaccurate and so – with the aid of a wind tunnel designed and built by themselves – they prepared their own. Their first glider, an original design, was completed in July, 1900, and by the end of 1902 they had progressed far enough to be ready for powered flight. No suitable power plant being available for their aircraft, they designed and built their own. It was crude and not very efficient, but it worked.

When they looked for design data on propellers, it appeared that nothing had been done in this direction, and after months of trial and argument they evolved

a very efficient airscrew for themselves. It was better, in fact, than anything else produced for some time. They grasped, too, the principle that a propeller was more efficient if geared down from engine speed.

Their gliding experiments took place at Kitty Hawk, North Carolina, where strong, steady winds enabled them to dispense with the need for natural or artificial launching hills. There they began assembling **Flyer I** (all their early powered aircraft were called "Flyer"), in September, 1903.

Mechanical problems and poor weather delayed the first flight until 17th December, when Orville made the first short hop. On the fourth (and last) that day, Wilbur flew 852 feet in 59 seconds, before rising winds wrecked the aircraft.

Their progress was rapid, considering the very short time they flew each year, and the brevity of each flight. On 20th September, 1904, Wilbur flew the world's first completely circular flight and on **Flyer III**, the 1905

aircraft, they were making flights of 24 miles and staying in the air for 38 minutes.

It was this 1905 **Flyer** that marked the peak of their achievements. It was the first really practical, controllable aeroplane and with it the brothers set out to commercialise their invention, offering it first to their own government.

To their chagrin, the US government was totally indifferent, and negotiations subsequently begun with Britain, France and Germany showed little more promise. Occupied with these frustrating and protracted manœuverings, the Wrights flew no more for three years, but in the interval continued their research.

Both of them were in Europe in 1907 and even shipped a **Flyer** there, but returned, leaving it in its crate, unused. In 1908, however, the success they sought was theirs. The American government, at last roused to interest, began to arrange purchase of Flyers after a convincing series of

demonstrations at Fort Myer by Orville – only slightly marred by a crash involving the first powered aircraft fatality.

That year, and early in 1909, Wilbur began a long programme of public flights in France, using the **Flyer** they had left behind in 1907. More than half of the flights were made with passengers. The effect of this on the French experimenters, whose progress had been on radically different lines and had become very slow, was remarkable.

It was the basis of the Wrights' theory of flight that an aircraft should be designed to be inherently unstable and that to achieve mastery of flight the pilot must learn positive control of his mount in all three axes. This led them, first, to the importance of lateral control, which they achieved by wing warping and, arising from inevitable aero-dynamic complications, to the vital necessity to co-ordinate lateral and directional control. This was perhaps their greatest contribution to the science of

flight. The early European inventors, mostly French, confronted with sufficient difficulties in getting their early aircraft airborne at all, preferred to avoid this problem by producing inherently stable machines. At the same time, while concentration on this prevented them initially from seeing the necessity of positive lateral – and directional – control, they discovered, as the Wrights at this time had not, the aerodynamic importance of a fixed tailplane.

It is understandable, after this, that the stunning demonstrations of absolute control in the air by the Wrights in 1908 should have caused the French considerable concern. The first tentative circular flight in Europe was as recent as November, 1907. Henry Farman, who made this flight, repeated it before witnesses (the French, unlike the single-minded Wrights, were very keen on official witnesses) in January, 1908.

This astonishment was heightened because, although

information on the Wrights' progress had been published from time to time in Europe, largely by Octave Chanute, the American gliding pioneer, it had been incomplete – although the message was there, for those who could read it. French attempts to follow the same lines were only moderately successful, leading to a feeling that the reports must be wrong, which only underlined the effect of the 1908 flights.

Once the French began to incorporate lateral control in their designs, however, their progress was rapid. Although the robust and simple **Flyers** remained popular (there were over 100 flying in the world in 1910), they were trickier, though initially more rewarding to fly than contemporary European designs. Surprisingly, they were still tied to the skid undercarriage and catapult-and-rail launching gear imposed on the Wrights by the soft sand and small, rough pastures of their 1903 and 1904 experiments.

The Precursors

4 The unique achievement of the Wrights was that they brought together successfully all the principles of powered flight. The possession of the internal combustion engine was their good fortune, for it turned their ideas into practicality. Most, if not all, of the principles had, however, been stated theoretically – and many proved practically – in the previous hundred years.

Sir George Cayley, an Englishman, set out between 1796 and 1809 all the requisites for powered flight. He sketched a very modern fixed wing aircraft, he flew a successful model and he investigated the behaviour of cambered wings, accurately setting forth their properties. He recorded discoveries on the movement of the centre of pressure of an aerofoil and on stability problems. About 1860, the French sea-captain J. M. le Bris, made a short gliding flight from a downhill launch, but all subsequent early experimenters, like Cayley, were brought up short by lack of suitable power.

Until the arrival of the internal combustion engine, brave efforts were made with steam-powered aircraft. About 1874, Félix du

Temple made the first powered take-off and another Frenchman, Clément Ader – the father of French aviation – became the first man to lift a powered aircraft from level ground.

Ader's later experiments, in 1897, with a complex and sophisticated aircraft, came to nothing as did Sir Hiram Maxim's 3½-ton steam giant in Kent, which generated lift, but would have been totally uncontrollable in free flight.

These were the men who solved, or almost solved, the problems of lift and propulsion (with steam) but who, for the most part, gave no thought to the next step – that of controlling their monsters in the air. That, as they say, came in a later lesson.

Three men now appear, in different countries, who are to direct the science of flight along its true path. Realising the basic fact that time spent in the air alone was valuable, and not yet within reach of a suitable engine, they turned to gliding.

Otto Lilienthal in Germany was the first man to make good and consistent gliding flights. Between 1891 and his death in a crash in 1896 he had

achieved glides of up to 750 feet and – far more important in its influence on others – had published detailed, comprehensive technical reports on what he had done.

Percy Pilcher, a young Scotsman, followed Lilienthal's lead in 1895, until he too was killed in a crash in 1899, while a far older man in the USA, Octave Chanute, began designing gliders at the age of sixty-four. Flown by younger men, they achieved considerable success. It was Chanute who perfected the light, strong, girder-truss biplane glider invented by Lilienthal and exercised considerable influence through his contributions to the technical literature of flight and his publicising the work of Lilienthal. A friend and supporter of the Wrights, he brought word of their successes to Europe.

At this same time, in Europe, one other man was struggling to the same goal. In 1901, Captain Ferdinand Ferber of the French army built a Lilienthal-type glider and later on, machines patterned on the published accounts of the Wright gliders. Although he obtained little success, he was an important link in European development.

Clément Ader remains, for France, "The Man who Gave the World Wings". There were no witnesses on the October day of 1890 at Armainvilliers when he claimed a hop of fifty feet in **Eole**, but there is no reason to suppose that it could not be true. Claims put forward later for the **Avion III**, that it flew nearly 1000 feet in 1897 do not seem to fit the quoted report of General of Engineers Mensier in charge of the official military commission to observe the attempts.

Lilienthal who wrote one of the classics of aerodynamics, *Bird Flight as the Basis for Aviation*, built five monoplane and two biplane gliders.

Percy Pilcher pursued his studies of gliding broadly on Lilienthal's lines, naming his four designs Bat, Beetle, Gull and Hawk. He, too, died in a crash; like Lilienthal, he was just beginning to investigate powered flight.

Octave Chanute, in the USA, perfected the biplane glider. His famous 1896 biplane, in the hands of A. M. Herring, made about 700 flights.

The Golden Age

It did not take the French long to recover from the long torpor of the early 1900s, once they had been shaken from it by the Wrights. They were the leaders of aeronautical thought in Europe – neither Britain nor Germany had achieved anything of note – and from the multiplicity of experimenters crowding the scene, four men now emerged to mould the creative years from 1908 to 1910. The two main lines of development were laid down in France: the pusher biplane and the tractor monoplane.

Gabriel Voisin, producer of the first practical European aeroplane, had been attracted to aviation by the work of Ferber. His cellular biplane was based on the boxkite invented in Australia by Lawrence Hargrave in 1893, with a second, stabilising tail cell and – like the Wright biplanes – forward elevators to control height. Modified and improved by Henry Farman, an Englishman living permanently in France, it became the definitive pusher biplane type.

Léon Levavasseur designed a number of light, reliable aero engines that produced ample power for a variety of aircraft. It was really these 30hp and 50hp motors, the latter weighing only 4·2lb/hp, that made flying practical. These Antoinette engines, with direct injection and evaporative cooling, powered a graceful, slender, efficient

monoplane of the same name, designed also by Levavasseur, which first appeared in 1908.

Louis Blériot, a contemporary, was also a monoplane designer. Diverted by a series of unpromising ideas, he did not settle to a practical design quite so soon, but his aircraft, although squat and uncouth beside the graceful **Antoinette**, were sturdy and successful.

It was sheer chance that decreed that it would be the Blériot and not the Antoinette that was to become the dominant monoplane type. On October, 1908, the London "Daily Mail" offered, as its fourth aviation prize, £500 for the first aeroplane crossing of the English Channel. It was not claimed that year, but the offer was repeated in 1909, this time at £1000.

By mid-summer, a number of pilots, including Wilbur Wright and his first French pupil, the Comte de Lambert, were contemplating attempts. The first to actually set out, on 19th July, was Hubert Latham, a popular and experienced Antoinette pilot, but his normally reliable engine failed him and he had to be rescued just short of mid-Channel by an attendant torpedo boat. Six days later, on 25th July, Blériot, flying one of his own

monoplanes, powered by a most inadequate three-cylinder Anzani of 25 doubtful hp, took off from Calais and landed beside Dover castle 36½ minutes later, just after five in the morning.

Latham tried again forty-eight hours later, for a French champagne prize offered in 1906 (for which Blériot had not entered in time) but his engine failed again, a mile from the English shore. The publicity for Blériot and his aircraft was enormous and so was the effect of this really epoch-making flight. It had the usual result upon military and official eyes of such occasions; it either opened them very wide indeed or sealed them tight shut. Nevertheless, there could be no denying that the two traditional defences of Britain, the Channel and the Fleet, had been effectively bypassed.

A month later, between 22nd to 29th August, the first great international flying meeting took place, sponsored by the champagne industry, at Reims. Twenty-three aircraft took part, including seven Voisins, with Wrights, Blériots and Antoinettes and a new and significant design by Louis Bréguet, who was to become an important figure in French aviation.

All the leading pilots were there, including Ferber (under the name of la Rue) and the American Glenn Curtiss, who had already begun to challenge the Wrights and was to outstrip them.

The impact of the meeting, coming so close on the heels of the Channel flight, was enormous. It gave very valuable publicity to flying as, before a distinguished audience headed by the President of the Republic, M. Faillières, records fell day by day. At the end of the week, flights of 112 miles had been made, and speeds of 48mph achieved, with heights of 508 feet.

At Reims, in 1909, Latham (*above*) pursues two biplane rivals on his **Antoinette VII**, repaired after its dip in the English Channel. On it, he won the Prix d'Altitude on 29th August with 155 meters.

Barely sustained at cliff-top height by his feeble engine, Blériot (*below*) searches anxiously for a gap to cross the Kentish coast at the triumphal climax of his cross-Channel flight. Wedged among the cross-bracing of the fuselage is the flotation bag added for the trip.

Powered by the 100-hp monosoupape Gnôme rotary, the **Avro 504** bomber eventually had one of the longest and most successful careers as a trainer of any aircraft in history, a number of later variants still being active in 1939.

The Salad Days

During the Reims meeting, Farman had re-engined his aircraft with a startling new motor. Designed by the Séguin brothers, it was a 50hp rotary – that is, the radially arranged cylinders revolved around a fixed crankshaft. Crude in conception though the whole thing was, it was very light, having no waterjackets or radiators, and ran at an efficiently cool temperature. Weighing no more than 2·7lb/hp, it survived until 1918 in more powerful forms. With such engines, aeroplanes grew steadily in reliability, reputation and respectability. Passenger flights became popular, and in 1910 the first woman learned to fly. One need hardly add that she was French.

f.8   Records tumbled, meetings multiplied and the conquest of the world by air, beginning with long-distance flights around and out of Europe, had begun.

The pioneers were beginning to be overshadowed by the second generation of designers. In France, Morane, Nieuport and Bréguet, whose aircraft were to help win the coming war, were now more prominent than Voisin, Blériot and Levavasseur. In Britain, the men whose names would become synonymous with the aircraft industry were building their first machines.

A. V. Roe, one of the great pioneers in England, developed a line of neat tractor biplanes, via the **Type 500** of 1912, that was to produce the most famous training aeroplane of all, the **Avro 504**. (Although it made history of another kind when three naval Avros bombed the Zeppelin sheds at Friedrichshaven with 20-pound bombs in November, 1914 – the first strategic air attack.)

The pusher was beginning to lose favour, but Maurice Farman, Henry's brother, introduced a big, gentle, cow-like design that was to serve almost every Allied nation as a primary trainer during the period between 1912 and 1917.

Unlikely though it may seem that the Maurice Farman pushers developed from the basic design of his brother Henry (*bottom left*), were ever military machines, they went to France on the outbreak of war with Nos 2, 4 and 6 Squadrons.

The **Maurice Farman** entered service with the RFC in 1913 and was universally known, from its spreading forward elevator structure (and undoubtedly from its bovine characteristics) as the longhorn. The **S.11** of 1914 (*upper right*), with the 100-hp Renault, appeared in larger numbers and as it lacked the forward elevator became the Shorthorn in popular terminology.

When the Wright-type forward elevator on its curving skids was removed, the two models became, inevitably, the "Long-horn" and the "Short-horn".

Geoffrey de Havilland, probably the most famous name in British aviation design, was beginning his career in 1912 with the **BE2**, a clean, very stable tractor biplane that would later equip many British squadrons. He worked at Farnborough, where the Army's Aircraft Factory was busy with technical developments and such aircraft as the 92mph **BS1**, the prototype of all fighting scouts.

Germany was also making rapid progress and her military flying, in particular, was well developed, despite the heady worship of the rigid airship as a weapon of war inspired by Count Zeppelin. Igor Etrich's **Taube** monoplane design of 1911 had been copied by many other designers, and some foreign designs built under licence, but the principal German developments from 1912 to 1914 were in the field of military two-seaters. Encouraged by competitions like the Kaiser-Preis and Prinz-Heinrich-Preis, sturdy biplanes with powerful, reliable four and six cylinder watercooled engines were available to train the German army in air reconnaissance.

Germany was reputed to possess 1000 military aircraft, France 1500. Britain, well behind, had 179 military aircraft all told.

Too much was done in this period to record it adequately here, but one event must be mentioned. The Schneider Trophy seaplane contest, started in 1913 at Monaco, and won by France, was to become the ultimate test of aircraft speed and a source of great international rivalry. Its effect on design was considerable and the 1914 contest was won by a little British **Sopwith** biplane. Those unaware of the progress made in Britain were surprised, but from this aircraft Tom Sopwith was to supply a line of famous fighting scouts.

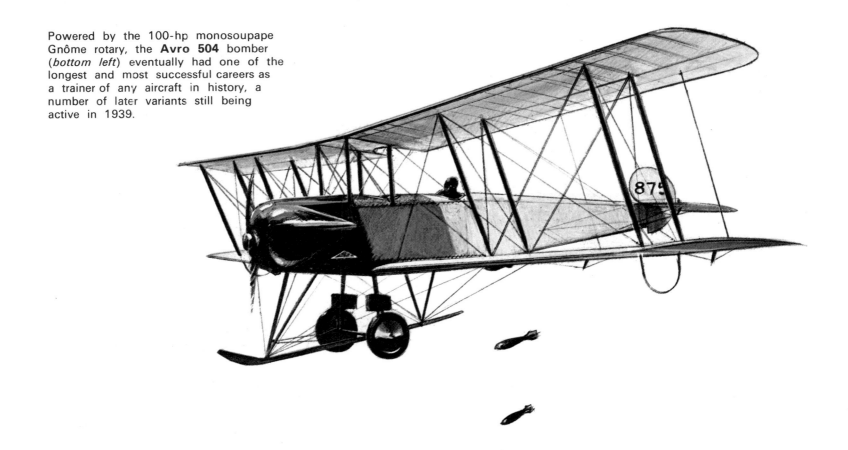

Powered by the 100-hp monosoupape Gnôme rotary, the **Avro 504** bomber (*bottom left*) eventually had one of the longest and most successful careers as a trainer of any aircraft in history, a number of later variants still being active in 1939.

13

Frail though the early **Zeppelins** sometimes proved to be, it is not difficult to see why their Gothic grandeur captured the imagination of the German people. This one, the military **Z IV** – seen over the Bodensee (Lake Constance) after her commissioning on 14th March, 1913 – survived until broken up in 1917.

Biggest of all the highly successful British pressure airships of 1914–1918, and one of the largest non-rigid ships ever built, was the 1916 **North Sea** type (*left*).

The Dirigibles

The story of the airship is incidental to the main story of powered flight, forming a separate historical line. Nevertheless, it is a part of the tale that ought not to be left out.

After initial successes in France by Giffard in 1852, the first practical non-rigid or pressure airships were flown by the Brazilian, Alberto Santos Dumont, at Paris and Monaco between 1898 and 1906. This inspired the development in France of numerous civil and military non-rigid and semi-rigid ships from Lebaudy, Astra and Zodiac, the main builders and, during the war, from the French government works at Chalais-Meudon. Design standards advanced considerably with the adoption by Astra in 1911 of the Torres system of internal bracing, producing strong, fast ships that formed the basis of most British wartime airships. Until the war started, the small

Willows non-rigids were the only real success, the bulk of military designs being uninspired and obsolete.

In Germany, on the other hand, thanks to the drive and tenacity of the elderly Count Zeppelin, the airship became a national symbol and ships of his design were to brighten the pages of civil airship history, as they were to darken significantly those of the war. His ships were rigids, the gas balloons that provided lift being contained in a framework of girders, covered with fabric. This was a great technical advance – the non-rigid airship, where gas pressure alone sustains the streamline shape, being very prone to drastic distortion of the envelope when gas was lost. (The semi-rigid type featured an added keel to stiffen the envelope.) The first Zeppelin – a name that rapidly came to symbolise all rigid dirigible airships – was built

in 1900. Despite crashes, failures and financial problems, the Count succeeded and there were 25 built or building by August, 1914.

Although they ran the world's first air service, these ships were intended for bombing and reconnaissance with the fleet and the army. When war came, they made admirable eyes for the High Seas Fleet, serving Scheer well at Jutland, but because of their vulnerability to weather and hostile action, were in the long run failures as bombers. They had quite a long run bombing England regularly through the first half of the war with considerable moral and material effect.

Of the 106 Zeppelins and 19 Schütte-Lanze rigids (the latter a wooden-framed ship) commissioned during the war, only six survived to be handed over to the Allies.

Ten British rigids of modest utility were built during the war, but a brilliant series of pressure

airships was used in anti-submarine, convoy and patrol work – largely at the instance of Admiral Fisher, who correctly guessed them to be a defensive weapon of great potency.

French work was confined to pressure ships, but their attempts to use them for tactical military tasks were inauspicious, and after 1916 some were handed over to the navy for coastal patrol.

In the United States, France and Britain, post-war development and rigid building programmes depended almost entirely on German practice, and after supplying several reparations ships, the Germans began to build again for themselves.

The Americans, French and British suffered a series of spectacular disasters, which eventually led to the shutting down of airship programmes. In 1930, the **R101**, launched in 1929 and with her sister ship **R100**,

Britain's greatest rigid, set out on her maiden voyage to India but crashed at Beauvais with the loss of most of the country's leading airship men. **R100**, which had flown successfully to Canada, was promptly scrapped, ending a dream of Empire airship commercial routes.

In Germany, the **Graf Zeppelin**, launched in 1929, was a complete success and was joined by the **Hindenburg** in 1936 on commercial operations. When the latter crashed in flames the following year in America, it marked the end of all effective airship operation, as **Graf Zeppelin II**, launched in 1938, was scrapped when war began.

Work continued in America with non-rigids designed by Goodyear, which repeated in the second World War the British success in the first. Now only a few non-rigids remain, for advertising purposes, and although

there is talk of reviving the big rigids in the 1970s, with modern techniques and safer gas, economic considerations make such construction unlikely.

The great rigids caught public imagination and although in the end they all failed, a look at their commercial record shows how near success they came. From 1909 to 1911 the French Compagnie Générale Transaérienne carried 2590 passengers on 273 flights; Delag, the commercial Zeppelin company, carried 35,000 people 170,000 miles between 1910 and 1914. By the end of 1932, Goodyear airships had flown over 100,000 passengers on 3500 flights, totalling 25,000 hours. **Graf Zeppelin**, by the same date, had made 290 cruises, carrying 7495 passengers. In 1929, she flew round the world and her record included 33 ocean crossings. All these commercial flights were made virtually without incident.

The Aeroplane Goes to War

On the Western front, at the start of the first World War, the German Air Service mustered, in terms of first-line (that is, reasonably serviceable) aircraft, some 250, disposed in 34 Fliegerabteilungen, each of nominally six machines. The French Aviation Militaire activated, on mobilisation in early July, 21 six-aircraft Escadrilles and two scouting Escadrilles de Cavallerie; a total of perhaps 130 aircraft. By October, following Commandant Barés's reorganisation, there were ten more squadrons and another scouting unit.

The British Royal Flying Corps, formed with a naval and military wing in 1912, mustered at Dover on 12th August to fly to France the next day. On that same day, Lieutenant Franz von Hiddeson dropped two light bombs from his Taube over Paris.

Numbers 2, 3, 4 and 5 Squadrons, RFC, settled into France over the next three days, losing four aircraft in the move, with 63 machines. Of the 116 left in Britain, none was remotely serviceable.

By reason of its limited performance, as well as the conviction of its military masters, the aeroplane in 1914 was considered fit only for reconnaissance and it rapidly proceeded to make its name in this task.

The RFC was used aggressively, even in the earliest stages. On 22nd August they plotted von Kluck's II Corps on the move round the north of the BEF, newly arrived at Mons.

Four days later, two French airmen made history with a voluntary reconnaissance over the Marne and found that the German II Corps had turned south short of Paris, exposing their flank.

The subsequent Battle of the Marne began on 6th September and on the 15th continuous trench systems put an end to the war of movement. Both sides now settled down to patrol, map, photograph and observe the front. The RFC adopted the system already in German use of operating squadrons under the orders of individual Army Corps, that became the basis of army co-operation work. In November, these squadrons were grouped into Wings and a year later the Wings made up Brigades. (It should be remembered that the RFC was administratively a Corps of the British Army.) At that same time, Army squadrons took up the work of protecting the Corps two-seaters.

The French already had their "cavalry" scouting squadrons and were beginning to exploit the single-seater – in units of one. French doctrine throughout the war tied its bombing and other squadrons closely to the army, operating as an extension to their artillery.

Early in October, the Germans formed two new Fliegerabteilungen, each of six **Fokker M8** two-seaters. Two of the basic concepts of air war were now established: the lone scout and the homogeneous squadron, operating a single type.

In November, the Germans began arming their two-seaters with machine guns, and as early as March, 1915, General Thomsen was reorganising the German Air Force into specialised squadrons with these aircraft and planning the introduction of large bombers. Those armed two-seaters, fashioned from the pre-war competitions, were to prove formidable opponents throughout the war.

A positive policy aimed at getting control of the air was

taking shape on each side. The aggressive armament of aeroplanes had been slow to start – largely because weight was critical. Before it was recognised that it was possible to fire guns forward without hitting the propeller, a Frenchman, Roland Garros, became the first "ace" by exploiting a device that simply deflected bullets from the blades of the airscrew. Crude though the device was, it allowed him to shoot down five unsuspecting victims before he was himself shot down and captured on 19th April, 1915.

His device, examined by the Germans, sparked off a working design for an interruptor gear from Fokker's factory and about two weeks later the first armed Fokker single-seaters arrived at the front.

They reached the front only slowly, and were scattered among the two-seater squadrons in the same manner as the French and British treated their scouts.

The **de Havilland** single seater, the **DH2**, reached the front on 31st July. Although it was promptly shot down, it was the first of the breed that was to defeat the Fokker. A nimble pusher biplane (the engine at the rear to obviate the requirement for an interruptor gear), it carried a single forward-firing machine gun like its opponent.

Although various interruptor or synchronising gears were available, none appeared to commend itself to the Allies, who continued to use the clumsy deflectors on Morane scouts. Even when the very advanced **Nieuport Type XI** French single-seater appeared during the summer, which was to start a period of French ascendency the next year, it carried a single Lewis gun mounted on the top wing on a complicated mounting, to keep the line of fire clear of the propeller.

It was Immelman who introduced the most significant change in tactics that summer, prompting the formation of three-aircraft fighting units, while the Allies were still allotting single-seaters on a scale of one or two per squadron.

Throughout July and August, the handful of Fokkers (25 at most at any one time) began to force the RFC to fight for its information and the stable but defenceless **BE**s that made up the bulk of the Corps squadrons began flying in pairs for some kind of protection. (The primitive mountings for observers' guns were of very little use.)

This German domination, thanks to exploitation of their lead in fighting scouts, continued through 1915 and was to remain until the Somme battles opened in the summer of 1916.

This portrayal of **BE 2** Number 347, the first RFC aircraft to land in France in 1914, conveys the solitariness of early military flying. The handful of **Fokker Eindecker** (*bottom*) achieved a reputation out of all proportion to their numbers in 1915–16. Principal users of the **Type N** or **Bullet** (*below*) in the RFC were 60 Squadron. A few went to 24 Squadron, whose main equipment was **DH2**s (*left*).

The Professionals

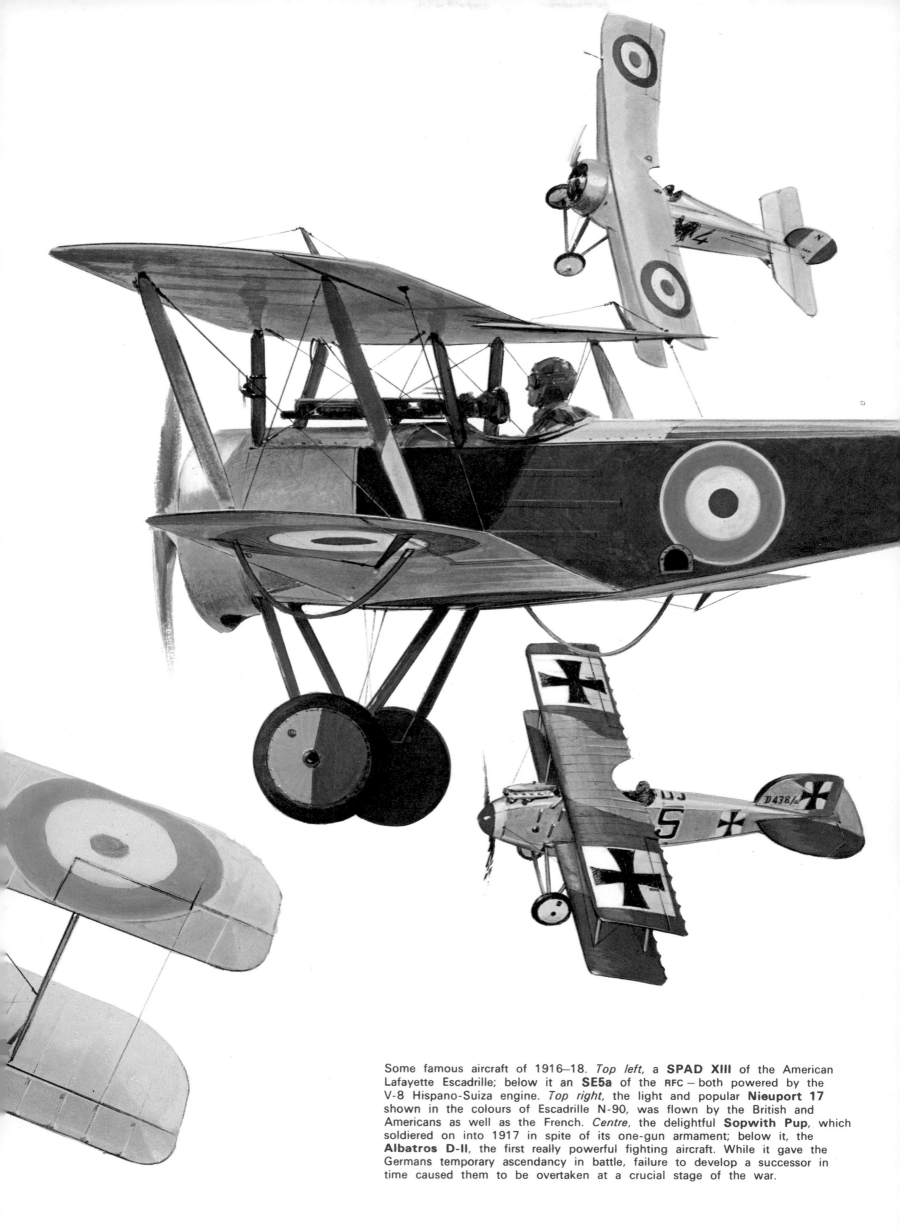

Some famous aircraft of 1916–18. *Top left*, a **SPAD XIII** of the American Lafayette Escadrille; below it an **SE5a** of the RFC – both powered by the V-8 Hispano-Suiza engine. *Top right*, the light and popular **Nieuport 17** shown in the colours of Escadrille N-90, was flown by the British and Americans as well as the French. *Centre*, the delightful **Sopwith Pup**, which soldiered on into 1917 in spite of its one-gun armament; below it, the **Albatros D-II**, the first really powerful fighting aircraft. While it gave the Germans temporary ascendancy in battle, failure to develop a successor in time caused them to be overtaken at a crucial stage of the war.

In January, 1916, proper formation flying began in the RFC, with fighting escorts to the two-seaters. In fact, there were now equal numbers of both types – 19 squadrons of each – on the Western front and the French were building up to a planned 119 squadrons. The new weapon of the fighting scout was forcing tactics to respond to its challenge.

On 2nd February, the first homogeneous single-seater squadron of the RFC, 24 Squadron, arrived with DH2s and, together with the Nieuport XI, had broken the Fokker's grip by the summer.

To counter these aircraft, the Germans introduced a most significant aeroplane, the **Albatros DI**. During 1916, the early Fokkers had been replaced by aircraft of similarly poor performance, which gave way to the Albatros in the autumn of 1916 in the German fighting squadrons, the Jagdstaffeln.

The Albatros was the first production two-gun fighter (two and even three guns had been tried on the Fokker monoplane experimentally), and the more powerful engine required to improve performance resulted in a new kind of aircraft. Bulky, heavier, and not so handy as the little rotary scouts, it required new thoughts on handling. Its stability as a gun platform and its duplicated armament, at a time when gun stoppages were frequent and targets fleeting, made it popular with pilots, but many were reluctant to make the change at first. Allied pilots such as Albert Ball, the RFC's first popular hero, found themselves uncomfortable initially behind the large stationary Hispano engines.

The Albatros regained for the Germans the initiative they had temporarily lost during the Somme battles and it was dominating the front in early 1917, the effectiveness of the German squadrons reaching a peak in "Bloody April". Throughout this period, the Allied fighting aircraft, **Sopwith Pups** and **Triplanes**, **Nieuport 17** and **SPAD S7** were single-gunned and it was not until the later **Sopwith Camel** and **SPAD S13** reached squadrons, with the excellent Farnborough-designed **SE5a**, that better performance and comparable armament swung the advantage to the Allies.

Initially, the Germans tried to counter this with even larger formations, forming the first Jagdgeschwader in July. It was

not, however, until the introduction of the **Fokker DVII** in April, 1918, during their last great offensive on the western front, that they made much impression.

With improvements suggested by their most famous fighting pilot, von Richthofen, it was an immediate success and within six months there were 800 serving in 48 Jagdstaffeln. It came too late to restore the balance against the Allies but was treated with considerable respect.

The development of bombing, like that of fighting, had been to some extent the result of tactical pressures on the battlefront. While the French were content to employ their bombers, **Caudrons** and **Voisins**, later replaced by the **Bréguet 14**, largely as a means to attack targets the guns could not reach, it was in this field that the RFC reflected and developed the aggressive and independent policies of their commander, Hugh Trenchard. The **DH4**, probably the best day bomber of the war, began to make longer and longer raids into German back areas, until very large running battles developed with the German fighter defence.

Credit for real strategic use of the air arm must, however, go to the Germans. Following the example of the successful Russian Sikorsky four-engined aircraft on the Eastern front, they initiated a programme of multi-engined aircraft for long-range bombing. Their giant aircraft, with up to six engines, were too advanced for their time and saw little employment in the west, but the twin-engined **Gotha**, which replaced the vulnerable Zeppelins on raids on Britain in the second half of the war, was more successful, although eventually forced to operate at night by stiffening defences, until the campaign had to be abandoned entirely in May, 1918.

It was reaction to the Gotha's success that decided the Air Board to adopt heavy night bombers. The Royal Naval Air Service in 1917 had been making significant strategic night raids with their tiny force of **Handley Page 0/100** patrol bombers, forming a special squadron to attack Germany in October.

This unit, "A" Squadron, joined 41st Wing RFC, formed for the same purpose at Ochey. An RFC development of the big Handley, the **0/400**, was produced early in

1918 and this composite unit was formed into the Independent Force RAF, dedicated to strategic bombing of Germany, in June.

The creation of the Royal Air Force had taken place, following the report of the Smuts Committee, on 1st April, 1918. Trenchard had been campaigning strenuously for a single, autonomous air force, able to form its own policies and operate in its own right on terms of equality with the army and navy. It will be seen later what effect this decision was to have on the development of naval aviation.

And then, suddenly, on 11th November, it was all over. The puny collections of aircraft of 1914 had swollen until there were 22,000 RAF and 15,000 German machines at the Armistice. There were 10,000 French effectives and the Americans, making their mark in the few months they were involved, had 740 aircraft in France, in 45 squadrons. Seventy-five per cent of these were French, the rest British. The creation of a huge air force overnight had turned out to be harder than their enthusiasm led them to believe, but five bombing and five observation squadrons flew American-built de Havillands.

The **DH4** was introduced into service with No. 55 Squadron in March, 1917, and marked a new era in air warfare. Designed by Geoffrey de Havilland as a day bomber fast enough to cope with enemy attacks on its own, its growing weight of bombardment attracted heavy opposition, and the tight formations of bombers were often escorted. The **Bristol Fighter** of 1917 (shown undertaking this task) was the most successful two-seater fighter of its time. Powered by Rolls-Royce, like the **DH4** its maximum speed of 119mph was good for its day and closely matched the 117mph of the bomber.

The fast-climbing, but fragile, **Fokker Triplane**, with a rotary engine, was never as successful as the brilliant **D-VII**.

The Explorers

The war left behind a great many pilots and a great many serviceable aeroplanes. Practically all of either category was available for employment in the cut-back to peace-time economics, but few found it.

France and Britain stored or dismantled their air fleets. In England, the Aircraft Disposal Company was formed, virtually to sell the assets of the RAF, whose very existence at this time was in grave doubt. The Americans, their own industry not yet born, cancelled the scores of ambitious contracts to build British or French warplanes. All three set out, through the Inter-Allied Control Commission, to smash every German aeroplane they could find – retarding much technical progress in the effort.

The world-wide spread of conflict had made ordinary people conscious of geography in a new way. And a great many flying men were imbued with a restlessness that now sought an outlet.

This feeling was focussed by the great aviation prizes offered almost as soon as fighting had ceased. The "Daily Mail" renewed its 1913 offer of £10,000 for the first direct Atlantic crossing, and the Australian Government offered a similar sum for the first of her servicemen to return home by air within a period of one month.

Although the first crossing of the Atlantic was made by a US Navy crew on board the **Curtiss** flying boat **NC-4**, it was a protracted affair with several stops and did not qualify for the great prize. This was won by John Alcock and Arthur Whitten-Brown, flying non-stop from Newfoundland to Ireland in a **Vickers Vimy** converted bomber on 14th–15th June, 1919.

It was another Vimy that made the most remarkable flight of the year, carrying two brothers, Ross and Keith Smith from Hounslow, England, to Darwin, Australia, between 12th November and 10th December, to win the Australian Government prize.

The **NC-4** (*above*) and the **Vimy** (*top*) of trans-Atlantic fame and (*centre*) one of the four **Douglas World Cruisers** that took US crews on the first round the world flight in 1924.

The Lonely Ones

There was a magic about the "non-stop" flight, the record-breaking attempt. The man who covered vast distances in a (probably) unreliable machine was always sure of the interest of both public and Press.

If he flew "solo" the effect was, of course, greatly increased. The man who really started the wave of solo flights was a young, small, quiet Australian, an ex-Squadron-Leader called Bert Hinkler. In 1920, he flew non-stop from London to Turin, over the Alps that were to claim his life in a later attempt, using a tiny **Avro Baby** with a pre-war 35hp Green engine. The flight took 9½ hours and he returned to England *via* Nice and Paris.

At this time, the true light aeroplane, symbolised by the **de Havilland Moth** of 1927, had not yet arrived and it was Hinkler's flight that did much to popularise this kind of flying. In 1928, in an astonishingly short time of 15½ days (half the time taken by Ross and Keith Smith) he made the first solo and first light aeroplane flight from England to Australia in an **Avro Avian**.

Up to 20th May, 1927, the North Atlantic had been crossed only twice by heavier-than-air craft. The most famous sea passage in the world, it was flown, solo, on 20th–21st May, 1927, by Charles Lindbergh, who landed at Paris 33½ hours after taking-off from New York. The flight, which won him the Raymond Orteig prize, made him famous overnight and caught public imagination as nothing else before or since.

In 1930, Amy Johnson leaped into public notice with a 19½-day London to Darwin solo flight – the first woman to do so. Her record stood until Jean Batten, a New Zealander, lowered the time to 14 days 23 hours 25 minutes in 1935, flying a **Percival Gull** and cut that to a splendid 5 days 21 hours 2 minutes in the following year. Fewer flights took place in the "uphill" direction; J. A. Mollison, later to marry Amy Johnson, flew from Wyndham to Pevensey Beach in 8 days 22 hours 19 minutes in 1931 and Broadbent reduced this seven years later to 5 days 4 hours 21 minutes.

In October, 1936, Jean Batten capped her career by flying solo from England to New Zealand in 11 days 1 hour 25 minutes, becoming at the same time the first woman to fly solo from Australia to New Zealand.

The South African route was to prove equally attractive to record-breaking pilots. Jim Mollison flew to the Cape in 4 days 17 hours 30 minutes in 1932 – to have his wife lop 10 hours 36 minutes off that the same year, but the most remarkable flight of them all, and the last great solo before the war, was Alex Henshaw's staggering London – Cape – London time of 4 days 10 hours in the tiny **Percival Mew Gull** in 1939.

From *top left*: Lindbergh's **Ryan NYP** Spirit of St Louis; Amy's **Moth** Jason; Hinkler's **Avian** and Francis Chichester's **Gipsy Moth**.

Following Lindbergh across the Atlantic, Amelia Earhart was the first woman solo pilot to achieve the flight, followed the same year by Jim Mollison's east-west crossing in 30 hours 15 minutes. This was the first solo light aeroplane flight and the first against the prevailing winds. In 1936, he crossed in the opposite direction on 30th October, in 13 hours 17 minutes in a **Bellanca Flash** instead of his Puss Moth. Earlier that year, on 4th–5th September, Mrs Beryl Markham reduced his east-west time by 8 hours 40 minutes.

In the Pacific, Francis Chichester, who had flown solo to Sydney in a leisurely 42 days in 1929–1930, made an astonishing flight from New Zealand to Australia, *via* the 5-mile-long Norfolk Island, 500 miles from New Zealand, and the even smaller Lord Howe Island, 575 miles further on. To have achieved these two landfalls was a most remarkable piece of navigation, alone in a DH Gipsy Moth.

The Trail Blazers

The **T-2** transport (*right*) used by Lt. Oakley Kelley and First Lt. John McReady to cross the USA in 26 hours, 50 minutes, 38⅗ seconds, on the 2nd-3rd May, 1923.

The **DH 50J** (*below*) on which Alan Cobham made his most famous flights was powered by a 385-hp Armstrong Siddeley Jaguar which gave it a cruising speed of 110mph.

The solo flights were only the most dramatic highlights of the great aeronautical expansion that took place in the 1920s and 1930s. Technically, a great deal of this early expansion was heroically ahead of its time; geographically, it followed a fairly logical pattern.

The United States, anxious to forget its foreign entanglements, turned its eyes inwards, within its own frontiers. The surface crossing of the continent was a sufficiently recent achievement to make the air "coast-to-coast" record a major goal. Much of the early record breaking and other pioneering flying was done by the US Services, strengthening a politically precarious position by positive propaganda wherever possible.

The natural goal of French ambitions was the linking up of her colonial empire by air, and just as British effort concentrated on long distance flights to India, Australia and South Africa, France sought pre-eminence around the Mediterranean, across North Africa and out to Indo-China. From West Africa, a natural extension led her to South America. Not only did the French sense an important market here, they were unable to expand initially to the south or south east, being blocked by British possessions.

One likes to think, too, that Santos Dumont, the gallant Brazilian who had set all Paris talking about flying before the war, was not entirely forgotten.

Overlaying all these natural pressures were the lure of the great distances and the great waters.

In America, an Army crew flew "round the rim" of the Union in 1919 and the first coast-to-coast attempt was made in 1921.

The first crossing inside 24 hours was made in 1922 by Lieutenant Jimmy Doolittle on a **DH4B** and the following year Lieutenants Kelly and Macready, flying the Army Air Service's big **Fokker T-2**, made the first non-stop coast-to-coast record. (Almost inevitably, the first woman to cross non-stop, in 1932, was Amelia Earhart.) It was another Fokker, a tri-motor **FVII/3m**, "Question Mark", that set up a flight-refuelled endurance record of 150 hours in 1929.

The Americans were among the earliest experimenters with this technique, developed and perfected by Sir Alan Cobham, the earliest pipeline refuelling record taking place in 1923.

The first trans-Pacific crossings were also made by the big, reliable, Dutch-designed Fokkers.

An Army **FVII/3m** flew from Oakland to Hawaii in 1927 and Charles Kingsford-Smith, most famous of all Australian pilots, made the first flight from the USA to Australia a year later. The first flight in the other direction, also by Kingsford-Smith, did not take place until 1934.

The name of Alan Cobham has become almost a synonym for the creation of the Empire air routes. After two trips to the Middle East, he flew the Director of Civil Aviation, Sir Sefton Brancker, to a conference in Rangoon in 1924, covered 16,000 miles to the Cape and back the following winter on a **DH 50J** and made the first out-and-back flight to Australia – 28,000 miles – in 1926, for which he was to receive knighthood.

He surveyed the England-South Africa commercial route with the **Short Singapore I** flying boat in 1927–1928 and took the big three engined **Short Valetta** to the Belgian Congo in 1931.

Up to the end of 1936, by which time the pioneering fever had begun to burn itself out and

commercial flying was building up, there were well over 100 successful (if occasionally rather protracted) flights, mostly in light aircraft, by British subjects round and about their Empire.

Royal Air Force units, their bases at great distances apart within that Empire, inevitably came into the picture. Unlike the Americans, still rather disturbed by the proselytizing zeal of Brigadier William Mitchell and anxious to "sell" the Air Services to their fellow-countrymen, the RAF gave little publicity to what it basically considered normal training.

Annual Cairo-Cape formation flights from 1926 and the later and much longer Far East cruises and early attempts on the long distance record were performed on ordinary Service machines, but the RAF did commission a special record-breaker, the **Fairey Long-Range Monoplane**, for a later long distance flight. The successful record distance of 5309 miles to South-West Africa in 1933 was beaten by the French seven months later.

René Couzinet's **Type 70** Arc-en-Ciel was a mail and freight carrier for the trans-Atlantic stage of the Aéropostale service to South America. Only one was built.

The Men of Commerce

One more long distance record was made by the RAF, with two of a flight of specially prepared **Vickers Wellesley** bombers, of the Long Range Development Flight, in 1938. They covered 7159 miles non-stop between Ismailia in Egypt and Darwin.

All this was in marked contrast to the flamboyance of the Italians, setting up a new military air power under Mussolini and anxious to impress the world. A series of spectacular and most successful long-distance formation flights were led by Marshal Italo Balbo. (Formation military flying for display was pioneered by the Italians.) Fourteen twin-hulled **Savoia-Marchetti SM55X** flying boats flew from Rome, over the Alps, *via* Northern Europe to Rio de Janeiro, traversing the whole length of the Eastern American seaboard. Two years later, in 1933, Balbo led 24 similar aircraft to the Chicago World's Fair from Rome, returning *via* New York, Canada and Portugal.

French activity in Africa and Madagascar led to a series of most meritorious record flights over the desert spaces in the 1920s. A special long distance version of the **Bréguet XIX** bomber was developed for what the euphorious French language called "les grands raids". The ultimate version of this famous aircraft became – and was officially called – a flying petrol tin, the Bréguet-bidon.

In 1925, Captain Arrachat flew non-stop from Paris to the Sahara in a **Bréguet XIXGR** and from Paris to Constantinople and back.

In 1927–1928 le Brix and Costes flew another one round the world. There was a number of French trans-Mediterranean flights, most of them on landplanes, for lack of a suitable flying boat.

Women were prominent in these pioneering flights. Amy Johnson and Jean Batten have already been mentioned. From France came Maryse Bastié, Maryse Hilsz and Hélène Boucher. It was a Frenchwoman, Adrienne Boland, who made the first flight across the Andes in 1921 in an aged **Caudron GIII** with 80hp engine. This flight was largely responsible for drawing the attention of the French to the possibilities of South America.

Between the first non-stop crossing of the Atlantic in 1919 and the first scheduled commercial services twenty years later, something like 150 attempts were made. The peak of this traffic came in 1927 and 1928, following Lindbergh's flight. A dozen crews disappeared in the years between 1927 and 1930, forcing governments to restrain the more foolhardy ventures.

The first east-west crossing was made by two Germans and an Irishman in 1928, and the first Paris-New York flight (the reverse of Lindbergh's) by Costes and Bellonte of France in 1930.

Two weeks after the Lindbergh flight, Chamberlin and Levine flew from New York into

Germany in the **Bellanca** monoplane "Miss Columbia". The big, load-carrying, steady Bellanca already held an endurance record and was the first aircraft to cross the Atlantic twice. Bellancas of different types made some dozen successful crossings in the next six years, but for some reason never achieved historical fame.

The **Fairey Long-Range Monoplane** (*top*) spanned 82 feet. Carrying 1000 gallons of fuel for its single 570-hp Napier Lion XIA, it could fly more than 5000 miles non-stop.

The **Bréguet XIX** was the hero of many French long-distance flights. Most famous of all, the much modified **Bréguet XIX GR** Point d'Intérrogation of Costes and Bellonte, redesigned as the XIX Super TR Bidon "flying petrol tank" (*centre*). It regained the World's Distance record for France in 1929 and made the first Paris–New York flight on 1st-2nd September, 1930. The **Dornier Wal** (*bottom*) began experimental trans-Atlantic services in 1933; Boreas, a production 10-ton **DoJ II Wal**, with 600-hp BMW VI, is shown on the Schwabenland's crane.

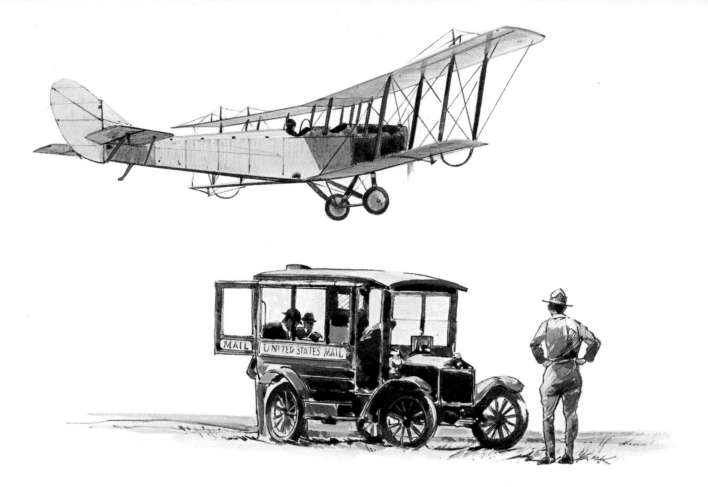

Between 1918 and 1921 the US Post Office developed a trans-continental air mail service between New York and San Francisco. The **Curtiss JN-4** followed a military training career during the war with a new lease of life as a stunt and mailplane.

The **DH-4A** (*right*) had a two-seat coupé cabin. 13 were employed by No 2 Communications Squadron in 86th Wing, RAF, to serve the Paris peace conference in 1919. Other **DH-4** and **DH-9** aircraft were modified and gave rise to the four-seat **DH-16** based on the **DH-9A** and the first real de Havilland airliners, the **DH-18** and **DH-50**. City of York, Instone's DH-4A in the picture, was winner of the first King's Cup Air Race in 1922.

For a number of excellent reasons, the earliest commercial services carried bags of mail, rather than passengers. The mailbag weighed less for a start, the risk of casualty was more tolerable and the bags suffered less from the unreliability of the service. Most important, when those first services ran briefly in England, France, India and America in 1911, the public would certainly not have supported anything so novel as an airline.

Early services were fragmentary and war soon put a stop to all civil development, but in May, 1917, the British government appointed a Civil Aerial Transport Committee to study future problems. The Committee reported on 7th February, 1918, on the need for state action to develop air lines and stressed the importance of surveying and setting up routes within the Empire. This preoccupation with Empire routes would later help to exclude Britain effectively from the lucrative European market.

The first regular services in Europe after the war were run by **DH 9s** of No. 1 Communication Squadron, RAF, flying mail to France and Germany and carrying officials to and from the Peace Conference in January, 1919.

In February, the first French Paris-London flight, with military passengers, took place with a **Farman Goliath** – a converted bomber. The first commercial air service was opened between London and Paris on 25th August, 1919, by Air Transport and Travel Ltd. On the same day, the first meeting of the International Air Traffic Association (IATA) was held, with airlines from Denmark, Sweden, Norway, Germany, Great Britain and Holland attending. Services across the Channel increased as other companies were formed.

At the end of 1920, the British lines ceased operation. The strain of competing against subsidised foreign airlines had proved too much. Shortly afterwards, the British government recognised in its turn that aid was necessary to launch the airlines and a subsidy scheme was operated between 19th March, 1921 and the end of March 1923. Wasteful competition among the companies involved led to a second scheme, on 1st October, for Daimler Airways, Instone Air Line, Handley Page Transport and British Marine Air Navigation, with specified routes for each.

All the early services, of whatever nationality, were operated with ex-military equipment, progressively modified to increase the comfort of the passenger – but not of the pilot. By 1922, a number of these ex-bombers, mostly single-engined, but with a proportion of twins, were beginning to show embryonic civilian tendencies. The twins, in particular, like the Farman Goliath and Vickers Vimy, had been given completely redesigned fuselages and the **Handley Page W8**, although demonstrably based on the 0/400 bomber, could almost be called a new design.

This dependence on converted aircraft (because they were much cheaper to acquire than brand new types) had the disagreeable consequence of delaying the introduction of new, genuinely civil designs. It also encouraged, partly as a result of the very narrow profit margins, the use of equipment chosen for a particular route (the choice being very wide) which led to an uneconomic number of different types being employed by one company. As the numerous small airlines in Europe tended, under economic pressures, to coalesce into single, national flag-carriers, the resulting fleets were, at first, anything but homogeneous and a maintenance nightmare. There were two aircraft, however, introduced into these early operations, that were destined to have a far-reaching effect on airline development.

One, the **Junkers F13**, came from Germany; the other, the **Fokker FII**, from Holland. Both were cabin monoplanes, the Junkers low-wing, the Fokker high. The German design was all-metal, Dr Junkers having pioneered this form of construction during the war. The Fokker was a welded steel tube structure (also standard practice in this firm during the war), built around the phenomenal high-lift wooden wing of Reinhold Platz.

Both types exhibited advanced characteristics and developed later into three-engined versions that shared the distinction of being the only European pre-1939 commercial aircraft to achieve substantial sales outside their own countries.

France and Britain continued to support their own industries, but, less sensibly, supported far too many separate firms so that the national airlines continued to operate small numbers of too many designs, uneconomic alike to builder and user.

The **F.13**, like other Junkers designs, was immensely strong and practically ageless. It served with airlines all over the world, including the USA and USSR and, with a three engined freighter development, the **G.31**, was responsible for opening up much of the wilder parts of the world to air – and consequently other – operations. A notable success in this field was the exploitation of the otherwise inaccessible natural resources of New Guinea.

The final passenger version, the Junkers **Ju 52/3m**, was probably built in larger numbers than any other European airliner of the period. Like many other German airliners of the 1930s, it doubled as bomber and military transport.

The Fokker progressed into the **F VII** and **F VII/3m**. Beside its use for many record-breaking attempts it, too, served many airlines and in the hands of the Dutch privately-owned national carrier, KLM, opened up the Far Eastern Dutch colonial routes to Batavia. KLM, founded by Albert Plesman in 1919, was the world's first national airline.

Apart from these two significant aircraft, the evolution of airliners proceeded slowly, with Imperial Airways, the British government airline formed from the merger of the subsidised companies in 1924, the most conservative of the lot. Imperial, the chosen

The Instone **Vickers Vimy Commercial** City of London (*top right*) was one of the most famous aircraft on European routes from 1920. The monoplane **Armstrong Whitworth Atalanta** replaced biplanes on the African route in 1933 (G-ABTL). The **Handley Page W.10**s like G-EBMM introduced cheap fares on European routes in 1927, while the luxurious **Armstrong Whitworth Argosies** (G-EBOZ) operated the Silver Wing lunch service to Paris. Later they went on to India, where the **de Havilland Hercules** (G-AARY) had been running extremely reliable services extended from the Middle East in 1930. **Hercules** also operated in Australia, where later, in 1934, QANTAS began using six **DH-86**s (VH-USE).

instrument of government policy, was committed by that policy to developing Empire routes. Because of problems of weather, limitations of daylight (passengers were landed for the night), difficulties in reaching agreement with foreign governments – notably Italy – for overflying rights and the introduction of new equipment, the routes changed frequently. Seasonal variations were common and until 1937 routes still contained sections covered by train or ship.

The longest route, to Australia, was completed in 1934–35, and the section from Singapore to Brisbane became the responsibility of Qantas, the Australian "flag" airline. The name perpetuates its origin in 1920 as the Queensland and Northern Territory Aerial Services.

France was opening up her own colonial empire routes, to Madagascar, Saigon and Africa. One of the most influential figures in this early development of French commercial aviation was René Latécoère. On 9th March, 1919, he had started the first regular mail service to Casablanca from Toulouse and formed his own airline, Compagnie des Lignes Aériennes Latécoère. His great dream was a French airline to South America and its achievement was one of the triumphs of airline history. Like many of the first airline operators, Latécoère was also an aircraft constructor and his own designs gradually replaced the converted wartime Bréguets that had worked the earliest routes and surveys.

Some of the greatest names in French aviation flew this difficult network: Guillaumet, Mermoz – who pioneered the trans-Andean section – and St. Exupéry, whose writing, in books like *Vol de Nuit*, provided valuable publicity.

An intriguing side issue of aviation history is the fact that only France made national heroes of her airline pilots, a fact which

In 1934 Imperial Airways put into service in Europe two **Short L.17**s, Syrinx (illustrated) and Scylla.

emphasises the importance the airlines played in her early development. By a similar curiosity, practically none of the German pioneer designers gave their names to the firms that they started. Not until the rise of Dornier, Heinkel and others in the 1920s did this individuality assert itself.

Lignes Aériennes Latécoère ceased operations in 1925, but the foundations had been laid. Aéropostale, formed in 1927 to continue the work, extended the line to Dakar and in 1928 made the first survey flight over the Andes.

Establishing this line proved tough. Aéropostale went into liquidation in 1931. In 1933, it was bought by the newly-established national airline, Air France, which had come into existence, like Imperial Airways, by the merger of existing companies. That year, Mermoz made the first commercial flight across the South Atlantic in the **Couzinet Arc-en-Ciel** (the ocean sector had been covered previously by fast mail steamers) and Air France commenced a through but rather leisurely air service. Arc-en-Ciel was an exceptionally clean, three-engined monoplane and a production aircraft of similar design, the **Dewoitine D.332** was accepted by Air France the same year, while Imperial had already received their first **Armstrong-Whitworth Atalanta**, a four-engined monoplane. The days of the biplane and the constructional methods that had not altered much since 1914 were numbered.

Even if the growing popularity of Junkers and Fokker aircraft was gradually imposing uniformity on airline equipment, national pride and internal competition meant that dreadful mixtures of types were still being operated on one route.

A similar national preference, largely for economic reasons, dictated the type of engines employed, but as most aircraft of the interwar period would happily accept any one of a number of similar engines, no installation problem existed.

As in most aeronautical development, the available power of motors dictated very largely

Most celebrated of all Imperial landplanes were the **Handley Page HP 42**s. These 95-mph giants entered service in 1932 and were still flying during the Second World War. Hannibal, portrayed here, was the first delivered of four Eastern models to work the Indian and African routes out of Cairo.

the design of commercial aircraft. Single-engined airliners endured as long as those with two would not stay in the air if one engine stopped. It was to overcome this safety problem that the three-engined airliner became so popular, although Imperial Airways, for whom safety was a more potent slogan than economy, standardised early on four-engined aircraft on scheduled routes.

There was the same diversity in the approach to operational methods by each national line. None operated under such curious conditions as the German line, Deutsche Luft Hansa, formed in 1926 after Deutsche Aero-Lloyd ceased operations.

Torn between national pride, her own rearmament problems and

the need not to be too obvious too early about this, Germany built up a concentration of national and international routes, using a multiplicity of equipment that bore no relation to her actual needs – having, in fact, a first-class network of roads and railways already.

This restored national morale, provided excellent basic military training when it could not be obtained openly and enabled several useful types of aircraft – not necessarily commercial – to be tested. Germany was busy reversing early history and turning out airliners that later converted with suspicious facility into bombers.

She no longer had a colonial empire as a goal for external

routes, but useful connections with the Soviet Union instead. Through this gap in the commercial barrier, Germany eventually completed an air service right through to Peking, fulfilling at last her classic "Drang nach Osten". German interests also began to challenge the French in South America, correctly sensing this to be an area of possible expansion, and several German-backed local airlines were started. From 1927, Deutsche Luft Hansa also began to set up operations over the Atlantic.

The story of German trans-Atlantic commercial flying is a fascinating one; certainly her methods were unique. From 1928 to 1937, the Luftschiffbau

Zeppelin and Deutsche Lufthansa (spelt thus from 1934) ran scheduled airship services to Recife, Brazil, from Friedrichshafen with the **Graf Zeppelin** (144 crossings) and the **Hindenburg** (a score of crossings, out of 63 flights). They worked the North Atlantic in summer, the South Atlantic in winter, with exemplary regularity.

In 1933, the catapult ship Westfalen came into operation at Bathurst, Gambia, employed to lift a heavily laden **Dornier Wal** into the air for the crossing to Natal. 328 crossings were made in this manner. In September 1936, eight trial crossings were made from another ship, Schwabenland, over the North Atlantic and a further 65 crossings made with this ship on the southern route in 1937–39.

Four-engined Blohm und Voss seaplanes were introduced on both services in 1937, and a four-engined flying boat, the **Dornier Do 26**, was designed for non-stop services to North America, but had completed only 18 mail runs by the outbreak of war.

In contrast to the flurry of activity in Europe, where aviation had had a sharp impact on daily life, the first regular scheduled airline in the USA, Ryan Airlines, did not begin operating until 1925. There had been local maritime services on a more or less regular basis before this, but otherwise the first seven post-war years saw only the Post Office Mail running across the country by 1921, and the Army's Model Airway, started in 1922 and coast-to-coast by 1926. Many sectors of the early British overseas routes were similarly run by the RAF.

It was not until 1925–26 that Congress passed legislation that enabled commercial air traffic to flourish. Two very significant factors of growth were the offering of air mail contracts and the development of the "lighted airway" – the father of all the navigational aids on which modern operations depend. Every airfield was equipped with powerful flashing beacons and lights were placed every three miles along the route between them. Threequarters of the transcontinental route was covered by 1926 and the whole completed in 1930.

From this period on, as in Europe, the giant airlines began to take shape, and with them the first generation of multi-engined

airliners.

One of the first in the field was William Boeing, who captured the prize western section of the trans-continental mail. A new and efficient **Mailplane**, designed and built by the aircraft company he founded, enabled him to underbid competitors.

The combination of aircraft-designer and airline operator was strong in America's formative period. Boeing later combined with Pratt and Whitney, who supplied his engines, and Hamilton Propellors, into United Aircraft. Later, the airlines were pried loose from these corporate manufacturers.

The battle for the trans-continental airway greatly influenced design in the 1928–32 period. Initially, passengers were regarded as rather a nuisance, income deriving mainly from the air mail contract, but Boeing had the foresight to build passenger seats into his **Mailplane** and one operator, Stout Air Lines, gave up its air mail contract because passengers paid better. (This was very significant and stemmed from the company's operating the **Ford**

Nearly 5000 of the **Junkers Ju 52/3m** were built, some of them continuing in military or civil use nearly 40 years after the prototype flew in 1932. During that time, almost every major European airline used them; Norwegian Air Lines (DNL) operated LN-DAF Najaden on floats, from 1936

Only two of the huge **Junkers G-38** were built, a step towards their designer's goal of a flying wing. D-2000/D-AZUR crashed in 1936, but the second, D-2500/D-APIS eventually became a troop transport and was destroyed by bombing in 1941. Another popular Junkers type, the **F-13**, was the first of all their commercial transports, dating from 1919. The example shown is K-SALB Bergfink of Finland's Aero O/Y. Below that is a **Farman Goliath**, a "civilianised" bomber of 1919 with which early French airlines began operations. Illustrated is F-ADDT Languedoc of Air Union. To the right of that is Air France's **Dewoitine D.338** Ville d'Angoulême of 1936 in front of the Bangkok terminal. Above it is the second of three **Savoia-Marchetti S.74**s built for Ala Littoria in 1935. The Italians gave considerable licence in registering aircraft euphonically, these three being I-URBE, I-ALPE and I-ROMA.

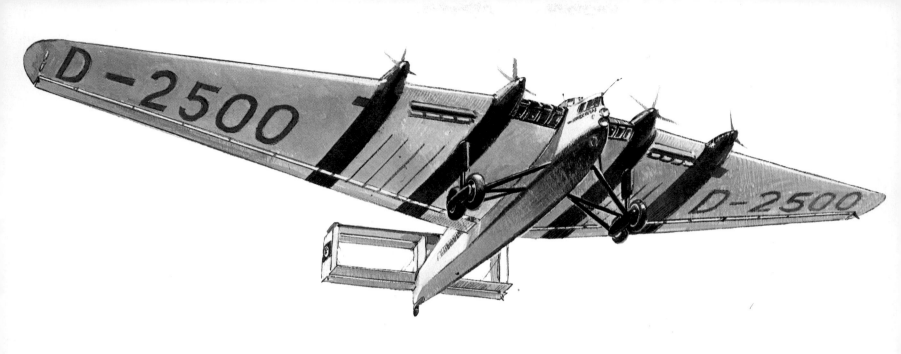

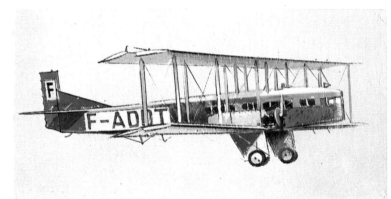

Another famous line started with the aircraft at the bottom of this page. This **Fokker F.VII** was one of five delivered to KLM in 1924–25 and developed into the well-known three-engined **F.VII/3m** of the same period.

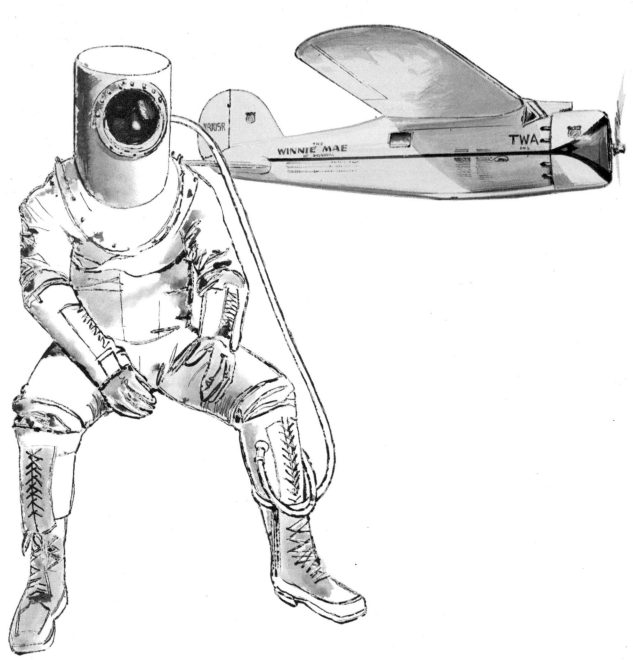

Experience at heights up to 25,000 feet in open aircraft in the First World War had led to the adoption shortly afterwards of oxygen-breathing apparatus, but it was to be many years before the general use of any but military or record-breaking aircraft at high altitude was to be considered feasible or necessary and little interest was shown in methods of making conditions bearable at great heights. For commercial purposes, it was obviously better to pressurise the whole cabin, rather than try to supply individual passengers with warmth and sea-level oxygen or pressure. The US Army Service tried out a pressure cabin in 1920 without success, and the cost, weight and design problems of such installations discouraged further effort. If successful cabin pressurisation had to wait until the **Boeing Stratoliner** of 1939, individual pressure suits for special purposes – the forerunners of the space suits of the 1960s and 1970s – arrived much earlier. One of the pioneers of these suits was American pilot Wiley Post. Best known for his record-breaking round-the-world flights, he successfully tried out the third of three suits designed to let him fly his **Lockheed Vega** Winnie Mae at heights of 30,000 to 50,000 feet in the England–Australia race of 1934. Although he did not compete, Post carried out valuable stratosphere flights with the suit (*above*).

For the Westland-Houston expedition of 1933, when the first flights over Everest were made (*left*), no pressure suits were available and the crews of the **Westland Wallace** and **PV-3** had to rely on oxygen masks (unsatisfactory because leakage lowered the effective pressure) and electrically-heated clothing.

Tri-motor, a metal version of the Fokker F.VII/3m, which set standards of comfort and reliability that made them very popular.)

By 1929, United had acquired three-quarters of the San Francisco-New York route. The battle for the remainder sharpened when the holder, National Air Transport, one that had rather despised passengers in the past, put into service the luxury **Curtiss Condor** twin-engined biplane. A classic financial struggle ended when United acquired NAT in May 1930.

Other rivals of United were working to complete a southern route across the States. Meticulously planned, with airway beacons, it had its own meteorological service. Pending the arrival of the **Curtiss Condor**, **Ford Tri-motors** were chosen as equipment, having the greatest public appeal. Commercial pressures were creating the infrastructure of airline operation and the "one type" fleet earlier than in Europe. At this stage, however, Transcontinental Air Transport, the operators of this route, still covered the toughest sections by surface transport.

Three famous aircraft of the mid-period of American air transport are pictured at Glendale Airport, California. In the foreground a **Ford Tri-motor** of Transcontinental and Western Air bears its Air Mail contract number, the key to successful operation. Behind it is a **Curtiss Condor** of American Airlines and overhead one of Boeing Air Transport's ten **Boeing Model 80A-1**s. An early Boeing attempt to produce a commercial transport from a military aircraft resulted in the **Model 307 Stratoliner**. A pressurised 33-passenger fuselage was mated to **B-17** wings and engines. Delivered to Pan American and TWA in 1939, they were taken over by the military for war duties.

The Last of the Big Boats

The beginnings of trans-Atlantic scheduled services, cut short by the Second World War, are symbolised in this picture (*below*) of a Pan American **Sikorsky Clipper** and Imperial Airways **Short C-class Empire flying boat** at Darrel's Island, Bermuda.

The three earlier flying boats (*above*) are, left to right, the **Short Calcutta**, flying the Nile sector of the African route in 1932, the French **Lioré et Olivier LeO H-242** of Air France's Mediterranean service (this is the prototype, Ville de Tunis) in 1934 and the giant, twelve-engined experimental **Dornier Do X** of 1929 — as unsuccessful commercially as most other aircraft of its kind.

The design and construction of large flying boats suitable for economical long-range commercial operation took time and money and waited upon the availability of powerful engines. The development, too, of suitable routes did not take place until war-surplus material was already obsolete, so no ready supply was at hand. Their introduction into civil operations dates, in fact, from about 1929.

In 1929, the largest aeroplane in the world was a flying boat: the twelve-engined German **Dornier Do X.**

In 1929, however, Imperial Airways began Mediterranean operations with their new luxurious **Short Calcuttas**; Aéropostale introduced **CAMS 53** and **Latécoère 32** flying boats in the same region and Pan American Airways, chosen as the national overseas airline of the United States, was cutting its

teeth on services round the Caribbean, but admittedly using flying boats only because of the lack of land bases. Lindbergh, who advised on the operation, strongly preferred landplanes.

The potentially lucrative Atlantic routes were still too tough for existing equipment, but two interesting catapult experiments took place, prior to the Luft Hansa services already described. When the Norddeutscher Lloyd liners Bremen and Europa went into service in 1929, each carried a catapult and a **Heinkel** seaplane which, launched at sea, took mail to New York ahead of the ship. With the later **Heinkel He 46**, launched 500–700 miles out from New York, the service cut 36 hours off delivery time from Europe. An experimental French service the same year, using a **CAMS 37** launched from the Compagnie Générale Transatlantique's Ile de France

saved 24 hours. (The first flight of this kind had been made by Chamberlin in 1927 with a landplane, flying off a platform on the American liner Leviathan.)

The growing Franco-German interest in South America spurred Pan American to rapid expansion of its flying boat services, partly by acquisition of other airlines. By 1932, they had a virtual monopoly and this, with the accumulated experience with boats over four years, made it possible for them to develop, with Sikorsky, the right aircraft for the routes. When the S-42 came into service in 1934 it was to set a new standard in luxury and technical advance.

It was in 1934 that the British Government announced the Empire Air Mail scheme, designed to carry mail along Empire routes with no surcharge. To implement this policy, Imperial Airways ordered a fleet of new four-engined flying boats from Shorts: the **C Class**, or **Empire**.

The French flying boat programme got under way more slowly. Crossings of the South Atlantic began in 1933, but were taken over by landplanes when the four-engined **Farmans** entered service in 1935. Two **Bréguet Saigon**, a flying-boat based on the **Short Rangoon**, appeared on Mediterranean routes in 1935, along with the **LeO 242**.

The graceful **Empire** boats started a regular Southampton-Alexandria service in February, 1937 and that year surveyed the routes to Australia, New Zealand, India and South Africa. A joint use of Bermuda as a flying boat base for Atlantic services was agreed between Britain and the US. (Bermuda was important in the long Southern route planned for winter operations.)

Simultaneous survey flights between New York and Bermuda, in opposite directions, were made by an Empire boat and an S-42 and long range versions of both types flew experimental trans-atlantic crossings in July.

In 1938 **C Class** aircraft took over the Singapore and Australia route. In July that year, in an interesting but short-lived experiment, the **Short-Mayo Composite** aircraft used a four-engined flying boat to lift a seaplane, heavy with the fuel for an Atlantic crossing and unable to get itself off the water by itself. The top component, **Mercury** flew non-stop from Ireland to Canada, her cargo of mail and newspapers giving this some claim to be the first commercial crossing by aeroplane.

Atlantic and Pacific open water routes were just coming onto a regular basis when World War 2 broke out and, as it spread, it gradually closed them down, although flying boats continued

to operate restricted overseas routes throughout the war, under military supervision.

On the Atlantic, the first Pan American mail schedule was flown on 20th May, 1939, the first passenger schedule on 28th June. The aircraft used was the new **Boeing 314**, a huge boat (it had the same wing and engines as the **XB-15**) in which American experience had put range, payload and comfort far ahead of its rivals.

Comparable French and British designs did not see the light until after the war.

Imperial started mail services on 5th August, with **C Class** aircraft, flight refuelled by Sir Alan Cobham to get the necessary range. Air France Atlantique, which made experimental crossings with the six engined **Latécoère 521** in 1938, had two operating in 1939.

In the Pacific, virtually an American preserve, PanAm set up scheduled flights to Manila with the **Martin 130** Clipper, completing the link to Hong Kong in 1937 with **Sikorsky S42**s. (Clipper was the company name for all their boats, regardless of

constructor.)

US domestic airlines, like everyone else's, grew to maturity on air mail contracts. Walter Brown, the Postmaster General, used the power given him by this gift to implement his plan for a healthy air transportation system, based on a few powerful airlines. In 1930, when contracts became renewable on a longer, ten-year basis, he quietly redistributed them among a "big four" of existing lines. This sound, if somewhat undemocratic, policy displeased those not involved in the shareout and after the change of administration in 1934 the "spoils conferences", as the shareouts were called, caused a scandal and the suspension of all airmail contracts. For a short while, the US Army, delighted to have the public eye, struggled valiantly to run an air mail system (possibly the only occasion on which domestic mail has been delivered by single-seater fighters) and later in the year fresh contracts were awarded.

They differed little from the originals. The "big four", United, TWA, American and Eastern, ran three transcontinental

routes and covered the eastern seaboard, while 16 smaller lines operated north-south routes, slung from a coast-to-coast system just below the Canadian border.

During this important development era, the stately **Tri-Motors** were being replaced by quite different aircraft. The **Lockheed Vega**, which set the pace, was a beautifully stream-lined, efficient monoplane, carrying six passengers at 135mph, which rose in later models to over 200mph. For a while, airlines followed the lure of speed (which was the only thing that compen-sated for the small seating capacity).

The small single-engined airliner was an anachronism, its demise hastened by the depression that swallowed most of the airlines using it, and in 1933 Boeing flew a most significant aircraft, twin-engined, all-metal and carrying ten passengers at 155mph. This was the **Model 247**, developed as a result of the **B-9** bomber.

In the hands of United Airlines, 30 **247**s cut the coast-to-coast time to under 20 hours in the summer of 1933.

An all-time great: the **Douglas DC-3**. United Airlines, committed to a fleet of **Boeing 247**s, could cope with **DC-2** competition, but had to buy the **DC-3** like everyone else.

The Dawn of Douglas

Design improvements and controllable-pitch airscrews put the cruising speed up to 190mph – well ahead of the **Tri-Motors** of TWA – and the ultimate fleet of 70 gave United a homogeneous fleet of the most modern airliner in the world.

Stung to action and unable to get **247**s themselves, because production was sewn tightly into the Boeing-United group, TWA wrote a specification for a design that was a step ahead.

It was picked up by Douglas, newcomers to transport aircraft, and translated into the **DC-1**. Developed into the production **DC-2**, it entered service in 1934, was faster than the Boeing and carried four more passengers. Unlike most manufacturers of the period, Douglas was tied to no airline and soon everyone – except United – was buying the **DC-2**. It became the biggest single factor in the development of air transport and cut Boeing out of the market until the arrival of the jets.

Foreign sales followed domestic ones, stimulated by the success of a KLM **DC-2** in the England-Australia race of 1934 which finished second overall and first in the handicap section, trailed symbolically by a **247**.

American Airlines, following the success of their Condor sleeper service, introduced a sleeper version of the Douglas, with bigger fuselage and more powerful engines. Sleepers were going out of fashion as speeds increased, but the 21-seater "day" version, the **DC-3**, was to become the most famous transport aircraft in the world. It dominated the American scene in the late 1930s and was beginning to interest other European users besides KLM, who were using it to replace their Fokkers on the Far East routes.

The Great Races

Of the half dozen or so big international air races that have taken place, the one that has always been The Great Race was the England-Australia race of October 1934. Conceived as part of the City of Melbourne Centenary celebrations and financed by Sir Macpherson Robertson (who liked to be called "MacRobertson"), the MacRobertson Trophy International Air Race rapidly became the only

part of the celebrations that anyone had heard of. The rules were drawn up by the Race Committee in Australia and the Royal Aero Club in London and contained two sections: a speed race, with £10,000 first prize and a £500 gold cup; and a handicap event with £2000 first prize. Pilots could enter for, but not win, both sections and although 16 days were allowed by the rules for the course, the winners were expected to do the distance in three or four.

The problems that beset any event of this kind brought the organisers at times close to despair. A seemingly endless row developed over the acceptance of American entries, because of differences in certification procedures. Only six weeks before the start was an aerodrome selected, a half-finished RAF base at Mildenhall in Suffolk with absolutely no facilities.

The entry list published in the third week of July contained 63 names from 13 countries. Although it was realised that this was padded by entries with no hope of either sponsor or aircraft, the eventual field of 21 was smaller than expected.

Algeria, France, Germany, India, Italy and Sweden, accounting for 12 entries, dropped out. Denmark and Eire, with one each, had no change. New Zealand lost one entry and Holland three of her hoped-for five and the three major blocks

of competitors, from Australia, Britain and the USA, suffered severely.

While eight of the 14 British entries remained, Australia was down to three from her original eight (Sir Charles Kingsford-Smith, her most famous pilot, was out) and only three Americans turned up from 18 listed.

Over-optimism, other commitments and sheer bad luck had restricted the entry, but enthusiasm for the race grew daily. The greatest interest centred on the big **Douglas DC-2** airliner of KLM, which very few people at the start had ever seen, calmly carrying a load of passengers and strongly favoured by those in the know, and on the three beautiful **de Havilland Comets**, dark horses so new that their crews were still getting used to them when the race started.

Interest in the race among British firms had been at best lukewarm and only de Havilland himself responded to the challenge, persuading his firm that they should take it up. It was a courageous decision. Time was short and they were very busy with normal work, but nine months before the race de Havilland announced a guaranteed price of £5000, promising a top speed of 200mph and a range of 3000 miles.

The courage was justified: three Comets were built and entered,

one by the formidable team of the Mollisons. It was C. W. A. Scott and T. Campbell Black, however – reaching Darwin in a shattering 2 days 4 hours 38 minutes in Comet "Grosvenor House", and knocking four and a half days off the record – who won the race.

They arrived at Melbourne 71 hours after leaving Mildenhall, first in both sections, with the big Douglas and Roscoe Turner's **Boeing 247D** second and third.

Scott and Black electing to claim the speed prize, the **DC-2** was declared first in the handicap section and in fact it was the achievement of the two airliners that had the greatest immediate effect on the aviation world, as Albert Plesman, the shrewd founder and head of KLM, had foreseen.

The dividend from the Comet's tremendous flight would not mature for another six or seven years, although the firm won well-merited publicity.

Nine other starters eventually arrived at Melbourne, the last in February, 1935. Crashes, forced landings and mechanical failures accounted for the rest.

The benefits to research and development and the publicity received from the big races are often quoted, but other competitions contributed equally to progress. These are the big international competitive rallies which, since World War 2, under

the leadership of the Fédération Aéronautique Internationale, have done much to sweep away the red tape that entangled international air touring. Before 1939, however, rallies were technically demanding and very competitive events, designed to test the skills of designers and pilots to the utmost.

The first of these contests was the 1925 Deutschlandflug or Rundflug. This was confined to German aircraft and pilots and was one of the great stimuli to their reviving industry.

From 1934, it became a highly professional team event and was the testing ground for the advanced, all-metal, retractable undercarriage **Bf 108**. This four-seat tourer from Messerschmitt was used to test components and features for the **Bf 109** fighter.

While up to 1933 the Rundflug had been a technical testing ground, it afterwards followed the pattern of the Challenge de Tourisme Internationale and other events and became a test of pilot ability. In the late 1930s, the Poles had consistent successes with light aircraft in these meetings, but sadly were to have no opportunity of exploiting them. German policies of promoting their aircraft industry and the Luftwaffe were evident, too. A team of prototypes of the Messerschmitt **Bf 109** took part in the 4th International Flying Meeting at Zürich in 1937 and swept the board.

The start of the great race to Australia. From the right, the Mollisons, in their **Comet** Black Magic which dropped out at Allahabad; Roscoe Turner's **Boeing 247D**; the two other **Comets**, those of Cathcart Jones and Waller (4th) and Scott and Black, the winners; and the **Douglas DC-3** flown by Parmentier and Moll.

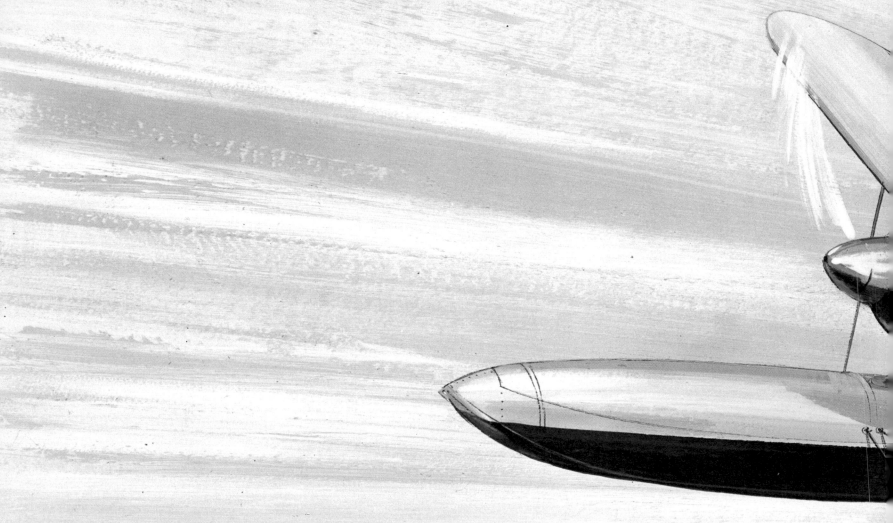

Apart from long-distance events such as the MacRobertson Trophy, there had been speed events for aircraft since very early days.

The first great international speed contest was for a trophy put up by Jacques Schneider in France for hydro-aeroplanes (the terms "seaplane" and "flying boat" had not yet been coined). Landplanes were excluded, because it was felt that the speeds that could be reached would require impossibly long aerodromes. Seaworthiness tests were included with the actual race, to stop freak machines from being entered.

The first round of what was to become the world's most famous speed contest was held at the hydroaeroplane meeting at Monaco in 1913 and was won by Prévost of France. The 1914 event was won for Britain by Howard Pixton on a little **Sopwith** seaplane giving the British their first real international success.

Britain, host nation as the current holders of the Trophy, organised the 1919 race. It was a complete fiasco. Seaworthiness trials were abandoned following damage to aircraft, and thick fog blanketed the course. The only finisher, an Italian, was disqualified when a mark boat reported failing to see him pass.

Subsequent races saw highly-specialised racing aircraft designed for the event and very high speeds were achieved. The us Navy-sponsored 1923 team began a general move to government backing for research and prestige/publicity purposes. Because of the time needed to design and prepare the aircraft, the race was made biennial in 1927.

In 1927 and 1929, the British government permitted an RAF High Speed Flight to represent the country, flying the beautiful and very fast **Supermarine** seaplanes designed by R. J. Mitchell. They won both contests and a third consecutive win would have given the holders the Trophy permanently. When the government refused, on grounds of economy, to sponsor a 1931 team, Lady Houston provided £100,000 to cover the cost. The use of the aircraft and pilots was sanctioned and on the **S6B,** a modified 1929 aircraft, Flight Lieutenant John Boothman won the race at 340mph. As no other nations had been able to produce teams, he had only to complete the course to win. Shortly after the race, the **S6B** set up a world's air speed record of 407mph.

There were air races at the Reims meeting in 1909, but the oldest race still in being is the British King's Cup Air Race, first flown in 1922. The most exciting series of races, undoubtedly, were those in the United States in the 1920s and 1930s for the Pulitzer, Bendix and Thompson Trophies. The Pulitzer ran from 1920 to 1925 and was the scene of intense rivalry between Army and Navy, testing standard military designs and specially-built racers. It was good for development, it was good for recruiting and it was a splendid way of presenting the air forces to the American public. When Service racing plans were dropped, the series finished but it had seen the introduction of many advanced features in aircraft which included clean metal monoplanes with retractable undercarriages.

From 1929, the annual National Air Races at Cleveland, Ohio, saw Service participation in standard aircraft, but civil entries

The Sea Fliers

During the First World War, both seaplanes and flying boats were developed for military work as the need for fleet scouts and anti-submarine aircraft became apparent, and ever-larger tracts of open water had to be patrolled. Offensively, where the Germans employed Zeppelins, the RNAS used seaplanes, and later landplanes when the former proved ineffective.

Germany developed sturdy fighting seaplanes for North Sea defence and nourished others on the quieter Baltic, but almost completely ignored the flying boat. The French built numbers of light, nimble flying boats for coastal work in the Mediterranean, and the Italians developed a series of fast, graceful little **Macchi** boats from a captured Austrian **Löhner**.

The British Admiralty had bought a number of **Curtiss** flying boats from America at the beginning of the war. The poor hull of the original was redesigned by Lieutenant Porte, resulting in a seaworthy design, the **Felixstowe F2A**, a vast but nimble boat of great range that could outfight the German fighting seaplanes.

The **F.5**, a developed **2A**, entered service in 1919 in Britain and America, with Curtiss producing the British-designed hull. It was a biplane, with two engines between the wings and open gun positions fore and aft. The **F.5** remained in service until 1925 and apart from the introduction of metal hulls to combat corrosion in the 1920s, subsequent British and American designs remained virtually

unchanged until 1937–38.

Although Britain pioneered the large patrol flying boat, introducing three and four-engined metal aircraft, some armed with a 37mm 1½-pounder gun, it was America that developed the theory of patrol employment most fully, using large numbers of big, twin-engined boats and smaller, general-purpose amphibians and flying boats for ship-shore liaison, transport and general tasks. Unlike the French and British navies, the US Navy controlled its own air force, which helped it to develop meaningful policies.

From 1925, the RAF relied on the **Supermarine Southampton**, similar to the **F.5** but with a more refined hull. Not finally retired until 1937, it served well in five or six Coastal Area

Enormous variety characterised the seaplanes and flying-boats of most air forces and navies. The diminutive **Fairey Flycatcher** from HMS Eagle, which served from 1923 to 1935 with the Fleet Air Arm, spanning less than 30 feet, is barely contemporary with the 90-foot-span **Short Singapore**, the first of which reached 230 Squadron at Pembroke Dock in April, 1935.

Behind the **Singapore** is a **Loening OL-8** observation amphibian. A late 1920s design, powered by a Pratt and Whitney Wasp, it became a real maid-of-all-work for the US Navy, engaged on arctic survey, communication and general fleet duties, including use as a taxi between aircraft carriers and the shore or other vessels.

The **CAMS 37** on the right is typical of the French naval flying boats of the 1930s. This aircraft, from Escadrille 3.S 1, was part of the non-embarked naval co-operation squadrons of the Armée de l'Air kept at the permanent disposition of the fleet.

squadrons, accomplishing in 1928 a 27,000 mile cruise from the Mediterranean to Australia and back.

In 1930, the RAF received the first **Blackburn Iris**, a big three-engined boat that introduced the very large, multi-engined long-range aircraft for ocean patrol. Followed by the four-engined **Singapore** and experimental six-engined **Sarafand**, both from Short Brothers, they gave the RAF invaluable experience for the **Sunderlands** in the war that was to follow.

Only a handful of these big, expensive boats was built in a period of national economic stringency. While 57 Southamptons were delivered, the whole production run of the 97-foot span, 14 ton Iris was *four* aircraft, and it took two years to

equip 209 Squadron with them. When this Squadron received the heavier **Perth** in replacement, only three were built.

Although the French Navy employed some flying boats, mostly conversions from graceful, four-engined civil machines, and built a version of the three-engined **Short Rangoon** under licence, they concentrated on smaller types and had a curious habit of putting land bombers on floats for coastal defence.

Italy used **Savoia-Marchetti** flying boats on her civil air

routes, and concentrated on fast, graceful, multi-engined seaplanes for naval purposes, largely confined to the Mediterranean and requiring less range. These were employed in record breaking attempts to advertise the new Air Force.

During the 1920s and 1930s, Japan began to develop her naval flying service, originally with the aid of a British mission. Confronted by the distances of the Pacific, she was to introduce large numbers of four-engined flying boats of very long range.

The Bold and the Beautiful

The great biplane fighters of the inter-war years. On the left, a **Curtiss BF2C-1** of VB-5 from USS RANGER flies over a Marines **Boeing F4B-3**. While the **Curtiss** was withdrawn in 1934 because of undercarriage trouble, **Grumman**'s success with a retracting-gear biplane fighter led to their replacing the **Boeings** from 1935.

In the right-hand column, the **Gloster Gamecock** (19 Squadron, *top left*) and the **Armstrong Whitworth Siskin IIIA** (41 Squadron, *top right*) were the first new fighters to replace wartime **Snipes** in 1923 and 1924. The next **Gloster** fighter, the **Gauntlet**, entered service in 1935 and in 1937 equipped 14 squadrons. It is shown in the colours of 46 Squadron, who re-formed with **Gauntlet II**s in 1936.

Prior to the 1937 **Gauntlet**, the most widely-used RAF fighter was the **Bristol Bulldog**. A pre-expansion aircraft, it entered service in 1929, replacing **Gamecocks** and **Siskins**. This one bears the red and blue squares of 23 Squadron. In the foreground, the 25 Squadron **Hawker Fury II** of 1937 shows off the lines of this magnificent 223-mph fighter. Hawker began building elegant biplanes to Sidney Camm's designs around Rolls Royce in-line engines in 1927; the **Fury II** was the latest and best.

Aviation in the twenty years of freedom from major war after 1919 was mostly dominated by the biplane. The slowing down of wartime urgency and the need for economies in national defence meant that the equipment currently in service remained there for several years. It was six years after the Armistice that new designs began to reach squadrons, and but for more powerful engines, metal propellers and metal airframes, these differed little from their predecessors for some time. Not until the mid-1930s did the monoplane begin to replace them.

Progress was further hindered by the political-economic struggle for control of the new arm. In Britain, thanks to the acceptance of the Smuts report, confirming Trenchard's advocacy of the "indivisibility of the air", the Royal Air Force, though under pressure from the other Services, survived intact. Created from the RFC and RNAS on 1st April, 1918, it at last became a force able to concentrate its effort, as it had been unable to do when the Army controlled half of its squadrons. It also took control of naval air operations away from the Admiralty, a decision of much less secure validity.

In the United States, apart from a brief independence for military aviation in 1918–1920, the principle that Army and Navy each controlled their separate air force was firmly established. Although inhibited by short sighted policies and inter-service jealousies, the United States Army Air Service (which became the Army Air Corps in 1926) was able to achieve a quality that was to see it through the war to come. The US Navy, in full control of its air arm, was able, in the years of peace, to develop the strategy and tactics that were to dominate naval warfare in the future.

The new Italian Air Force, created as an independent Service by the Fascist government in 1923, developed along lines largely dictated by political and prestige considerations. The German Air Force had, for the moment, disappeared, to be recreated later.

The shattering blows that France had sustained during the war left her with a difficult recovery and imposed a defensive policy and attitude on her forces. French aviation was still firmly in the hands of the General Staff and even after public pressure had helped to create an independent force in 1933, following the setting up of an Air Ministry in 1928, that independence was only retained by

relinquishing control of marine flying largely to the navy. This reduced the potency of the Armée de l'Air.

Progress in fighting aircraft hangs very greatly on the availability of reliable, powerful power units. In 1919, the British aircraft that could have fought a successful war or guarded a victorious peace were designed around the **ABC Dragonfly**, of which 11,000 were on order. Unfortunately, the Dragonfly was a disastrous failure. There was no alternative engine, many promising prototypes died and the RAF had to soldier on with the rotary-engined **Sopwith Snipe** until the first successful post-war radial, the **Armstrong-Siddeley Jaguar**, was fitted to new designs in 1924–1926.

The re-appearance of a German air force in 1935 had been a surprise to most people. Permitted to retain a small army for internal security purposes in 1919, the Germans concealed in it a camouflaged air department and began to rebuild their air force. By 1925, using a secret base in Russia at Lipetsk, they were training personnel and testing new aircraft.

In 1933, when the Nazis came to power, Lipetsk was abandoned and an Air Ministry created in

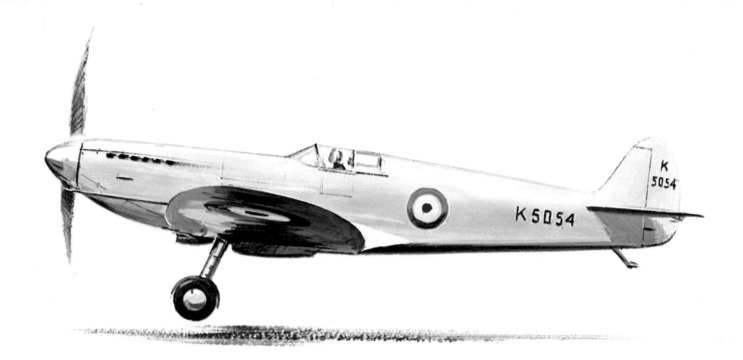

The **Boeing Model 248** was designed in 1931. From the signing of a contract for three prototypes in December, 1931, to the first flight on 20th March, 1932 (construction began in January) was a creditably short time. Serving through 1934–40 in seven Pursuit Groups, the stubby monoplane became a popular symbol in its colourful markings. The aircraft shown is from the 94th Pursuit Squadron, 1st Pursuit Group. Under its service

designation of **P-26** it is significant because it convinced the Army, following the unsuccessful **Boeing XP-9**, of the value of the monoplane, and is interesting for another reason. Boeing already had practical experience of cantilever wings and retractable undercarriages at this time; the retention of fixed gear, braced wings and open cockpit on the **P-26** would seem to be an example of military conservatism. Nevertheless, it weighed less than 40lb more than its biplane predecessor and was nearly 30mph faster on only 20 extra horsepower.

The **P-26** was the first tentative step towards the modern fighter. The **Hawker Hurricane** was the next. Though it was a more decisive step forward, being designed some three years later, its biplane origins are shown in the original name of "Fury monoplane" attached to it. It followed the classic structural methods of the biplanes, whereas the **Spitfire** (*above*), fractionally later in time but much more advanced in concept, was the first British example of all-metal, semi-monocoque construction. The first **Hurricanes** reached 111 Squadron in December, 1937, the first **Spitfires** going to 19 Squadron in July, 1938.

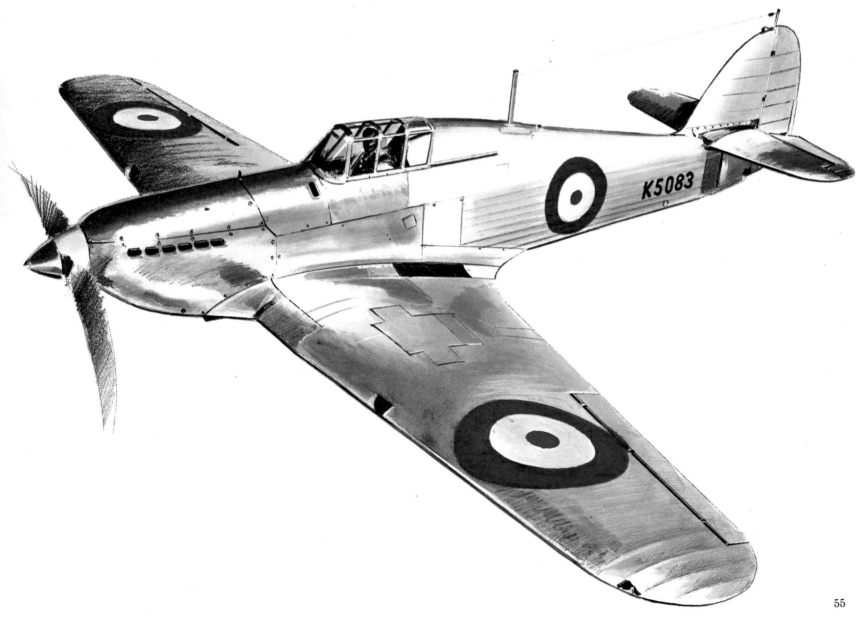

The Bombers

Sombre and ungainly in its Nivo green camouflage, the **Handley Page Heyford**, which replaced the vintage **Vickers Virginia** in 1933, served the RAF in 11 heavy bomber squadrons until the arrival of the monoplane **Whitleys** and **Wellesleys** in 1937. The last biplane heavy bomber in the British service, its only other claim to fame was having taken part in the first radar defence trials.

As the **Fury II** was the last, so was the graceful **Hart** the first of the **Hawker** aircraft designed round the Rolls Royce Kestrel. The squadron shown, No 33, were first to receive the type in 1930, followed by 18 other units, including eight Auxiliary Squadrons. The **Hart** was fast and manœuvrable but it really represented the ultimate in 1918 military thinking.

Germany. Following a reactivation period, the Luftwaffe, as the new force was called, came into the open in 1935 and began a series of rapid build-ups and regroupings.

Initial fighter development, at Lipetsk, had been orthodox, but when the rapid expansion began in the later 1930s, the Germans were, although hampered by the secrecy previously necessary, unfettered by either obsolete policies or obsolete aircraft. In fact, in the **Bf 109**, they were first in the field with a modern fighter. It first flew in 1935, six months before the Spitfire, and although its designer had no previous experience in fighters, most of the technical problems involving flaps, retractable undercarriage and leading edge slots and other parts had been worked out in the civil **Bf 108**.

In common with the Italians and Russians, the Germans tested their military aircraft extensively in the Spanish Civil War of 1936–39. They set up a complete miniature air force including anti-aircraft units, and evolved methods of operating their new equipment.

Both the **Bf 109** and the biplane **Heinkel He 51**, with which the Germans perfected ground attack methods, were tested in this way.

Reliable liquid-cooled engines like the French **Hispano-Suiza** and the American **Liberty** (once its early troubles had been

The **Martin B-10** represented a new kind of philosophy, with its enclosed gun turret and cockpits, internal bomb stowage and clean monoplane lines. Faster, at 210mph, than the fighters of 1933, it was ordered promptly by the US Army Air Corps.

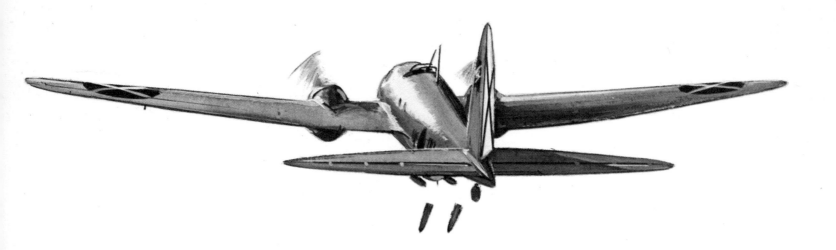

overcome) were available. They were bulky and heavy, however, compared to radials, and their cooling system was vulnerable. For this reason, after 1928, the USA concentrated on radial engines. In Britain, following the heavy Jaguar, came the light and admirable **Bristol Jupiter** of 1925, first of a line of excellent radial engines that were built widely under licence abroad. The **Gloster Gamecock**, powered by the **Jupiter**, had a top speed of 145mph at 10,000 feet.

Three months after 23 Squadron received the first Gamecocks, the cause of the liquid-cooled engine was revived by Richard Fairey's **Fox**, five mph faster at the same height. There were two interesting facts involved in this: the engine was the American **Curtiss D-12**, developed from the Navy racing engines in Schneider Trophy aircraft; and the Fox was a two-seater bomber. Financial restrictions prevented the Fox from reaching more than that one squadron (who lorded it over the annual air exercises for several years) but Fairey had shown what could be done by careful streamlining in design, and with the advent of the **Rolls-Royce Kestrel** in the 207-mph **Hawker Fury** of 1930, the liquid-cooled in-line dominated RAF fighter design until the advent of the jet

American fighter design was stimulated by the intense rivalry both between manufacturers (also competing on the airlines) and between the Services (already competing on the football field). It was further advanced by competition on the races of the 1920s.

Boeing and Curtiss competed for military orders, the first Boeing Army fighter, the 150-mph **PW-9** of 1925 having the Curtiss D-12 engine, although they afterwards switched to Pratt and Whitney radials (like Boeing, part of United Aircraft), reaching 190mph with the 1929 **P-12**. Thereafter, Boeing mostly provided Navy fighters, while Curtiss supplied the Army almost exclusively, basing its designs on the firm's successful record-breaking and racing seaplanes, and switching to radial engines after the 1929, 192mph **P-6E**.

The biplane, with its low wing-loading and small size, remained popular for a long time. The RAF had not completed conversion of its squadrons to the monoplane **Spitfire** and **Hurricane** by 1939, but with increases in power and speed and new techniques in construction, the biplane was bound to give way to the low-drag monoplane eventually.

The last of the major powers to abandon the biplane was Italy. The Regia Aeronautica was committed to a "window-dressing" policy that put a premium on manœuvrability in spectacular aerobatics – for which biplanes were well suited – and in addition, Italian pilots were notoriously conservative, resisting closed cockpits, for instance, even when they received modern monoplanes.

Monoplane fighters were introduced in America with the advanced **Boeing P-26** of 1933. This was a wire-braced, fixed-undercarriage design. In spite of retractable-gear, closed-cockpit, cantilever monoplanes having been

developed in the 1920s on racers, the USAAF did not receive their first machines with these features until 1938, by which time Hurricanes and Spitfires were entering squadron service in the RAF and the **Messerschmitt Bf 109** had been in service – and in action, in Spain – for a year.

In one respect, Americans fell far behind contemporary thought. In 1937–38, when the Hurricane and Spitfire carried eight rifle-calibre machine guns and the Bf 109 was beginning to appear with two 20mm cannon and two machine guns, the **P-35** and **P-36** carried only two machine-guns each, mounted on the cowling, where they could be reached by the pilot to clear jams (a relic of a 1917 problem) but where synchronising gear slowed down their rate of fire.

Technical development of bombers followed similar paths to that of fighters and flying boats, the fast monoplane replacing the vintage biplanes in 1937–38. The policies of their employment however, were rather more complex.

From the First World War emerged the two concepts of slow, heavy, multi-engined bombers, operating strategically at night (that is, on targets divorced from immediate battlefield needs); and faster, single-engined day bombers in tight formation, hacking their way at great expense through defending fighters, but always getting through to the target. The bomber, in fact, was the offensive arm of the air service, the fighter the defensive – a generally held theory strengthened by various prophets of universal air war in the 1920s and 1930s.

The RAF fought bloodless repetitions of the 1914–18 war in the annual air exercises and employed itself more lethally, and even more unrealistically, in small wars on tribal opponents of the Empire. The French and Italians did the same.

While they may have been an admirable method of keeping order, air operations in colonial wars led their practitioners to develop "general purpose" or "bomber-transport" designs quite useless in the face of any opposition. The French, in particular, based their first air policies in 1933 on the "multiplace de combat", a kind of aerial tank theory that gave way to the BCR formula (Bombardement, Combat, Renseignement), which sought a design to bomb, fight or reconnoitre and double as a transport. It bred a series of lumbering monsters of almost total ineffectiveness.

Not until the 1950s did experience and technology combine to produce effective multi-role combat aircraft. Pursuit of the ideal in 1930 merely coloured policies and influenced equipment in the wrong way.

While the defensively-minded US paid little heed to the bomber in the first ten years of peace, it was there that the first significant forward steps were taken with the B-9 and B-10 in 1931–33.

Boeing's B-9 gave the US Army Air Service the first all-metal, monoplane, monocoque fast bomber. Twin-engined, with retractable undercarriage, a small number were ordered. The big order, however, placed when financial conditions were better, went to Martin's B-10, which featured additionally an enclosed gun turret and a bomb load carried wholly internally. Boeing countered this advanced aircraft in 1935 with a giant step forward to the B-17.

Four-engined, supercharged for high altitude operation and with five enclosed gun-positions, it achieved 290mph in the service version. It was typical of the American scene that the initial order was drastically cut for political reasons. The bomber was designed for coastal and overseas defence, which the Navy claimed was their prerogative.

The first clean monoplanes entered RAF bomber service in 1937, the **Bristol Blenheim** replacing the last twin-engined biplane, the **Handley-Page Heyford**. Like the Fox before it, the Blenheim, first delivered to 114 Squadron, outran contemporary fighters, but, with the single-engined **Fairey Battle** that replaced the **Hawker Hind**, was obsolescent when war broke out in 1939.

Two famous pre-war bombers that were almost unique in giving continuous front-line service until the end of hostilities are seen here in their early versions. Two Staffel of the **Heinkel He-111B** were formed early in 1937 in K.88, the bomber Gruppe of the Legion Condor, to evaluate the type during the Spanish civil war. Despite its poor defensive armament of three 7·62mm MG 15 machine guns and low power (880/850-hp Daimler Benz DB 600C), it did well against feeble fighter opposition and deluded the Germans into thinking that the design was defensively adequate.

A similar fate awaited the **Vickers Armstrong Wellington**, shown with the original manual one-gun nose and tail positions. Although these were replaced by two-gun or four-gun Frazer-Nash power turrets and, the retractable ventral turret gave way to beam guns, the **Wellington** proved no more able to defend itself in daylight than the other day bombers. Unlike them, however, its excellent design and tough geodetic construction ensured its survival in the bomber squadrons.

The Fight for Naval Air

Lieutenant G. C. Colmore, RN, became the first naval officer to learn to fly, gaining his Certificate on 21st June, 1910 and four other officers of the Royal Navy began a course of instruction on 2nd March, 1911 – thanks to the generosity of private citizens.

The operation of aircraft off ships began when Eugene Ely, a civilian test pilot with Curtiss, took off from a 120 foot platform on USS Birmingham in a 50hp **Curtiss** landplane on 14th November, 1910.

On 9th May, 1912, Lieutenant Gregory, RN, made the first take-off from the deck of a moving ship, HMS Hibernia, and on 12th November Lieutenant Ellyson, USN, made the first catapult launch with the **Curtiss AH-3** in Washington Navy Yard.

In spite of early feeling in the Royal Navy that the development of aeroplanes would weaken British superiority in ships – a prophetic thought – progress in building an air arm was rapid, naval aircraft bases being established in 1912, and HMS Hermes, a 5600-ton cruiser built in 1898, being converted in 1913 to carry two Short seaplanes aft and a Caudron forward on a crude launching platform. At the same time, conversion of a collier to carry seaplanes for overside launching was undertaken.

The constitution of the Royal Flying Corps on 13th April, 1912, envisaged naval and military wings and a Central Flying School. On 13th May, it took over from the Balloon Battalion, Royal Engineers, and acquired the 16 naval aircraft.

From the outset, the Royal Navy regarded this arrangement with suspicion (the RFC was, after all, an Army unit) and continued quietly to run its own school at Eastchurch and arranged to procure its own aircraft. In fact, on 1st July, the polite fiction of the Naval Wing was dropped and the Royal Naval Air Service became an established fact.

The RNAS pioneered strategic bombing, struggled valiantly to operate the fragile seaplanes of the day with the fleet and against the enemy and gradually evolved the aircraft carrier from the clumsy seaplane mother ships of 1914–16.

The Eastchurch Wing, transported to the Mediterranean for the Gallipoli landings, tried out wireless communication, spotted for ships' guns and successfully torpedoed two Turkish merchant ships. (The first successful torpedo drop was made on 28th July, 1914.)

They bombed ships and hunted submarines and from the Air Stations along the North Sea coast fought savage running battles with the German Marine-Fliegerabteilung's small but efficient seaplane force.

On 1st April, 1918, with the creation of the RAF from the RFC and RNAS, the Admiralty lost control of its air arm for 20 years.

The flying boat squadrons became part of the Coastal Area, RAF, and embarked flights formed

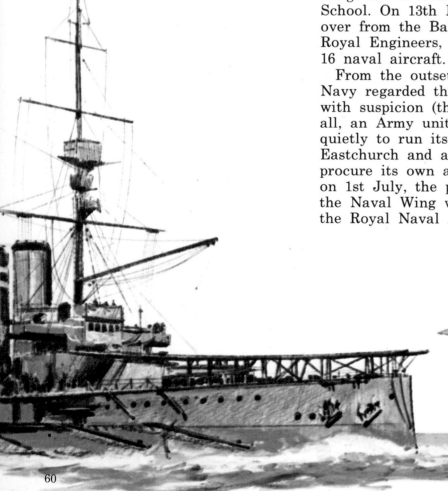

Lt. Gregory (*below*) flew his **Short S.27** from the bows of HMS Hibernia 27 years before the **Swordfish** seen leaving HMS Courageous in 1939 (*above right*), but the aircraft did not seem to have progressed as fast as they might. The **Swordfish** had a theoretical top speed of less than 140mph, but it was to be a long time before anything better was supplied.

the Fleet Air Arm of the Royal Air Force.

As early as November, 1915, experiments on HMS Aurora proved that it was possible to launch scouts from warships and from June, 1917, air cover for the fleet was provided by aircraft flown from indecently short, removable platforms over the guns of battleships and cruisers. It was in the development of the aircraft carrier, however, that the RNAS's chief claim to fame was to lie, even though it took an inordinate time.

Between 1913 and 1916, the Admiralty commissioned no less than ten seaplane carriers. Six had take-off decks but they were rarely used. Campania, the largest and most active, used hers only for seaplanes, launched from wheeled dollies.

The first landplane take-off was made from HMS Vindex as early as 3rd November, 1915, but the first landing came two years later, on 2nd August, 1917, on HMS Furious.

Five carriers were commissioned in the 1920s, which were semi-obsolete by 1939. HMS Ark Royal, launched in 1938, was the Royal Navy's only modern ship of this type.

The US Navy had six carriers, and from the introduction of the giant USS Lexington and Saratoga in 1929, carrying 90 aircraft apiece to Ark Royal's 70 and the 20–30 of the older British carriers, it began to work out the strategy of the powerful, carrier-orientated, independent task force.

In the 1929 fleet exercises (an attack on the Panama Canal), Rear Admiral J. M. Reeves employed Saratoga in a prophetic rôle, sending her on a long, independent sweep to the south of the main fleets and scoring a decisive victory over the defence.

This thinking was sharpened by the sinister expansion of Japanese naval air power – they had 10 carriers at the time of Pearl Harbour – while outside the Pacific, Britain had to take account only of the solitary French carrier Béarn.

France, her interests centred largely on the Mediterranean, felt less need of embarked air power and was, moreover, experiencing the same struggle for control of naval aircraft as in Britain. The formation of the French Air Ministry in 1928 set off a fight for control of maritime aviation that was resolved by a famous "air-marine" truce in 1932, between Georges Leygues, Minister of Marine, and Paul Painlevé, Minister of Air. This gave control of embarked aviation to the navy, of coastal flying boats to the Armée de l'Air (but on "permanent loan" to the navy) and left a small, specialised land force of marine-orientated fighters and bombers as part of the Army air force. All this made for a complex and unhappy arrangement.

A very dissimilar agreement was made in Britain between Trenchard, Chief of the Air Staff, and Keyes, deputy to Beatty, the First Sea Lord, in 1924. This was a step towards increasing naval participation in control of the Fleet Air Arm, which had been assigned to the RAF in the Balfour report, and was basically a way of implementing it in practice. Finally, the Inskip report handed back control of shipborne aviation to the Navy in 1937.

The Men of the North

While men were linking the continents and opening up the air routes between the major centres of the world, there was developing, in Northern Canada and in Alaska, the most specialised flying of all, as men employed the aeroplane to penetrate the northern wildernesses, up to and into the Arctic Circle.

The "bush pilot", flying on floats in summer and on skis in winter, was the new American frontiersman. He had no airways and no beacons. Initially he had no radio either. When he wanted maps, aerodromes, fuel dumps and weather forecasts he made his own. His flying was in virgin territory, in treacherous and extreme weather. He learned to navigate in the most bewildering landmarks in the world, close to the magnetic pole. And, as he carried out the fruits of their labours, he brought to the surveyors, the miners, the trappers and the prospectors the very means of their existence. He carried into the north the missionary, the doctor and the policeman, as well as ever-increasing trade.

The first flight into the North-West Territories of Canada took place on 2nd March, 1921, when two **Junkers F-13**s on skis flew to Upper Hay River. On the Eastern side of the continent,

Sidney Cotton was operating into Labrador from Newfoundland with **Martinsydes**.

In 1927, mail flying began in the Yukon Territory. By the end of the decade, regular operations and a host of private "bus-routes", often on a one-man/one-'plane basis, were spreading North and West. The aircraft included commercial **Fokkers**, **Bellancas** and **Lockheeds**, but more often one of the big, single-engined **Fairchild** monoplanes, in a variety of models. Their big, reliable radial engines pulled them in and out of the most inaccessible spots and kept going in sub-zero conditions that made maintenance the most laborious

in the world.

The development of civilisation in Alaska meant widespread use of the aeroplane. Physically separated from the USA and with no native transport system, the use of the air was vital. The first experimental flights into the Territory in 1924 gave birth, in 1928, to Alaska Airways. Later a subsidiary of Pan-American, it built up the life of Alaska with its operations.

The part played by aviation in Alaska has never diminished. By the 1960s, the State had the largest number of aircraft per head of population anywhere in the world.

One of the aircraft that helped to open up the Canadian north-west was the **Fokker Super Universal**. Fokker's unique skills in welded steel tube construction gained him a foothold in the United States, where he formed the Atlantic Aircraft Corporation, whose first product was the Universal. Robert Noorduyn, the general manager, later produced his own design, the **Norseman**, to fulfil a similar purpose.

The Second Round

The **Gloster Gladiator** was the last RAF biplane fighter, and two squadrons fought in the Battle of France, one in the Battle of Britain. Other **Gladiator** squadrons saw very active service in Norway and the Middle East and Greece. The picture shows (*top right*) one of Malta's **Gladiators** dog-fighting with an Italian **Fiat CR 42** high above the island.

The early **Hurricane** (*below right*), despite its poorer performance, was available in far greater numbers than the more sophisticated **Spitfire**. In the Battle of Britain it destroyed more enemy aircraft than all other defences together.

The years between the arrival of the first **Bf 109B**s in Spain in the spring of 1937 (to restore the initiative to the Legion Condor) and the closing shots of the Battle of Britain were crucial in the story of air warfare. In those years all the tactics were worked out, the strategies established – for good or ill – and the promises that had been faintly foreshadowed in 1916–18 were fulfilled.

When the Germans flung the 1581 combat aircraft of Luftflotten 1 and 4 across the Polish border on 1st September, 1939, they started the first full-scale air war in history. Like Jutland, it will probably remain unique.

Although the fighter forces attracted, naturally, much more public attention than bombers, they were universally regarded as being a purely defensive arm. The bomber was the offensive weapon of any air force; the fighter was there to parry its thrust, to intercept or pursue it. While the Americans, concentrating entirely on their proposed long-range bomber force in the late 1930s, allowed fighter development to atrophy, European nations, with swift hostile bomber fleets at their doors, developed fast, powerfully-armed single-seaters.

The Germans had the great planning advantage of knowing the mission that their air force was to fulfil, and they provided a completely mobile supply and base organisation to accompany the Luftflotten in mobile warfare.

They had also profited from the lessons of Spain, at any rate where fighters were concerned, and evolved the combat formation based on two loosely linked pairs, with No 2 in each case responsible only for protecting his leader's tail. This formation, as the "finger four", was to become universal coinage in the jet age (the pair is still the basic unit today), but in 1940 the British and French clung to their impressive but unwieldy peacetime close formations. The RAF finally "loosened up" during the Battle of Britain.

The composition of the German invasion force in Poland reflected current thinking, with 897 bombers to 210 fighters (mostly the **Bf 109**, but with a few twin engined **Bf 110**) and 470 transport and reconnaissance aircraft. To these the Poles could oppose only 159 semi-obsolete fighters in a total air strength of just 397 aircraft.

It was the Poles, not their

opponents, who were the heroes of the fighting. 327 of their whole force were destroyed (98 escaping to Rumania), but their fighters shot down 78 bombers, 79 fighters and 31 dive-bombers before being overwhelmed. In all, the Germans lost 285 aircraft. The Poles, alert to the imminent threat, had dispersed their fighters to prepared emergency fields on the eve of invasion and so avoided being caught by the heavy bombing of their peacetime airfields. Unfortunately, this and other lessons did not reach (or did not impress) the other Allies. The lessons that were presented were by courtesy of the Germans who had filmed, in monotonous detail, the savage destruction of Poland. This epic, *Baptism of Fire*, was shown to a selected diplomatic audience in Oslo just before that country was invaded.

The brief Norwegian campaign brought home to Britain a basic fact of modern war: he who holds the air usually wins the battle. Against the advice of the Air Staff, who had a very clear notion of the consequences, the invasion was disputed with practically no air cover. Political expediency and lack of flying effectives caused this folly to be frequently repeated during the war. In the case of Norway, the British army and navy suffered heavy losses, including the precious aircraft carrier HMS Glorious. On board her when she went down were the remnants of

46 Squadron and their **Hurricanes** and the survivors of 263 Squadron, whose **Gladiator** biplanes had accounted for 50 enemy aircraft before they had been themselves destroyed, mostly on the ground. While the Norwegian campaign was yet in progress, the Germans fell upon France.

In 1936 a vast new production scheme, the "shadow factory" system, was started, and this timely effort, matched by a parallel increase in training and recruiting, meant that the RAF was at least adequately, if not luxuriously, equipped with modern fighters by early 1940.

Not so in France. Her rearmament programme started very late. Plan V, calling for 34 Groupes of fighters in Metropolitan France, with about 750 aircraft, was formed in 1938. But when the Battle of France opened on 10th May, 1940, she had built only 420 single-engined fighters to oppose the 1346 **Bf 109**s, 355 **Bf 110** and 1615 bombers that the Luftwaffe could call upon. Only two of the 24 Groupes, with **Dewoitine 520**s, were fit to match the Messer-

schmitts, though an additional four Groupes of American **Curtiss Hawks** were a useful asset.

Although the French had worked out a scheme for reinforcement of threatened sectors, their Armée de l'Air was still fatally attached to ground Armies in separate sections that could not be readily redeployed.

On mobilisation, it became obvious that no effective infrastructure of ground communication and transport existed, and when the front broke on 15th May, this flaw destroyed them almost as surely as the weight of the Luftwaffe did. Thirty per cent of the French effectives were lost in the month's fighting.

Four squadrons of **Hurricanes** were based in France on 10th May. As the fighting progressed, more and more reinforcements were sent after the original 60 aircraft, to try to bolster the defence. Air Chief Marshal Dowding, C-in-C Fighter Command, seeing clearly what lay ahead, fought to keep his precious aircraft in Britain, but 261 – the equivalent of 13 squadrons – were committed before he could call a halt.

(*Top*) The Soviet **Yak-3** was an outstanding fighter at altitude. (*Centre*) The **Lockheed Lightning** long-range fighter served on almost every battlefront. (*Bottom*) The **Mitsubishi A6M Reisen**, the Zero, dispelled any us hopes that Japan was backward in fighter design. (*Centre*) Castoldi developed his **Macchi C.200** from Schneider Trophy designs, but it needed the German Daimler-Benz engine to become competitive.

The **Spitfire V** was outclassed by the excellent **Focke-Wulf FW190** (*top*) over 20,000 of which were built, but was ahead of the 1940 **Messerschmitt Bf109E** (*upper right*). The **Thunderbolt** (*right*) was a massive fighter with great fire power (8 0·50 machine guns). This one is an 8th Air Force escort aircraft of 353rd Fighter Group. Only a handful of the 600 **Dewoitine D520** on order ever saw battle. This one was with GCIII/6, 5th Escadrille, in 1940.

When that battle was over, and Dunkirk was done, 432 **Hurricanes** and **Spitfires** had been lost.

The Battle of Britain was a classic air engagement on fairly equal terms as far as quality was concerned. Quantitatively, the Germans could muster 1031 fighters and 1259 bombers against 749 British fighters (figures for 10th August): but they had lost the advantage of surprise and the RAF were operating from firm home bases.

This time, the bombers came more heavily escorted by fighters, because the destruction of the RAF fighter force was the objective. Dowding, and Keith Park, commanding 11 Group, which bore the brunt of the battle, fought so skilfully despite critical wastage of pilots and aircraft that the escorts were forced onto the defensive. On 16th August, of 1720 German aircraft attacking southern England, 1300 were fighters.

Altogether, the Battle of Britain cost the Luftwaffe 1733 aircraft destroyed and 2500 valuable aircrew killed or taken prisoner, for an RAF loss of 1118 machines.

Many tactical truths were learned or relearnt in these significant opening battles. Perhaps the most significant fact, was the complete lack in any air force of a competent long-range escort fighter. This had restricted German attacks to south-eastern England in 1940 and, as will be seen, it severely hampered Allied operations for the first three and a half years of the war.

After the Battle of Britain, RAF Fighter Command found itself forced into its opponent's rôle, when a series of fighter sweeps into France were undertaken in order to strike at the enemy. Up to the German invasion of the Soviet Union in June 1941, 104 small and 11 large sweeps produced 26 enemy casualties for 33 RAF aircraft lost. Intensified operations in the next six weeks to try to divert German fighters back from Russia did not succeed. Only 200 German fighters remained in France and even the loss of 81 of these (for 123 RAF aircraft shot down) did not ease matters in the east.

The Offensive Weapon

Nothing that had happened since 1918 had given any air staff in Europe or America in 1939 cause to believe that daylight bombardment – the offensive essence of an air force – could not be carried out unescorted. German experience in Spain came nearest to providing the truth, but opposition had been slight, and the Polish campaign, where Geschwadern of 80 to 90 Heinkel **He 111** might be under the escort of a solitary Staffel of nine **Bf 110**, did little to disillusion the Luftwaffe.

Poland proved so successful in making the tactical liaison between bombers and ground troops that the Luftwaffe became identified by its end as a tactical force – a process begun before the war, with the death in an aircrash on 3rd June 1936, of General Wever, the proponent of German strategic bombing, and the ensuing abandonment of four-engined bomber development in favour of more rapidly-produced tactical types.

RAF enlightenment came more quickly. Faced with shockingly high casualties in early actions against the German air fleet, the elderly **Whitleys** were quickly

USAF conceptions of its mission hung on strategic bombardment, centred on the **B-17** force in 1943–44. Symbolic is this **Boeing B-17G-DL** Douglas-built at Long Beach, serialled 44-6508 and serving with 401st Bomber Group of the 8th Air Force in Britain. Many considered that concentration on this mission atrophied fighter development, but the **North American P-51 Mustang**, which became one of the most famous fighters in the world and incorporated lessons learned by the RAF in two years of war, was healthy enough. This **P-51-NA** of 374th Fighter Squadron, 361st Fighter Group at Little Walden, was one of 8th Air Force's escort force for the bomber formations.

relegated to pamphlet-dropping at night, to be followed by the faster, but uncomfortable and under-gunned **Hampdens**. Even the **Wellington**, an admirable bomber that served with distinction throughout the war, proved no exception, once the German fighters had found its weak points.

Daylight operations became restricted to raids on occupied France at distances susceptible to fighter protection, but fortunately British aircraft and crews were readily adaptable to night bombing.

The United States Eighth Air Force came to Britain as part of the build-up for a planned invasion of the continent in late 1942 and early 1943. Code-named "Bolero", this policy followed Anglo-American agreement that

Germany, not Japan, was to be the first priority as a target.

Strategic bombardment, for which the USAAF had been fashioned, was planned to be the primary weapon in destroying that target, and from June, 1942, the Eighth Air Force began to build up its strength in heavy and medium bombardment Groups.

The 97th Bombardment Group flew the first mission on 17th August, 1942. In eleven missions, under Spitfire escort and so of short distance, only two **B-17s** were lost. The first results looked promising.

At this point, conflicting requirements for the limited number of "heavies" available caused most of the Eighth Air Force's effectives to be transferred to the Twelfth, supporting the North African landings. This and

other depletions reduced it to between two and six Groups until the summer of 1943.

Although this force was too small to give decisive results or effectively prove its cause, long distance raids in the period taught the vulnerability of the **B-17** to head-on attack and saw the introduction of tight-packed, close-stacked "combat boxes" to counter the growing aggressiveness of the Luftwaffe fighters, amounting eventually to a force of some 700.

In August, reinforced to twelve-Group proportions, the Eighth made an historic attack on the anniversary of its first raid, sending 376 aircraft deep into Germany, unescorted, to Schweinfurt and Regensburg.

(*Above*) US medium bombers struck repeatedly through Japanese defenses to destroy port installations and sink shipping. Here, in a typical attack, a **B-25 Mitchell** sweeps across Rabaul harbour, New Guinea. (*Below right*) a **Bristol Blenheim IV** of 105 Squadron; though better than the **Battles** the squadron took to France in 1939, the **Blenheim** could not defend itself without fighter escort. (*Below left*) the **Avro Lancaster** was to become the chief weapon of Bomber Command, able to carry the 12,000-lb Tallboy and 22,000-lb Grand Slam bombs. 149 Squadron, one of whose **Lancasters** is shown here, came late to the type, in September, 1944, *via* the **Wellington** and the **Stirling**.

The bomber version of the versatile **de Havilland Mosquito**. The **Mk IX**, one of which is seen coming in to land, featured the bulged bomb bay doors to enable it to carry a 4000-lb bomb.

Despite the apparent evidence of its circular cowlings, the **Junkers Ju 88** was powered by Jumo V-12 in-line engines of 1300hp, giving it a maximum speed of over 300mph (*top*).

Saddest and most desperate of all the shifts to which fighting aircraft were put were the various kamikaze suicide adaptations of Japanese fighters and bombers. Here a modified **Mitsubishi G4M2a Betty** (*bottom*) releases an **MXY7** Navy suicide attack aircraft.

They lost 60 four-engined bombers in day-long, running attacks, but continued operations and on 14th October again sent a strike against Schweinfurt. Out of 291 aircraft another 60 were shot down.

Such losses were insupportable, but fortunately for daylight bombardment (if not for the enemy) the answer to the problem became available in December with the arrival of the first long-range **P-51 Mustang** escorts.

The belated adoption of drop-tanks had provided the **P-51**, **P-47** and **P-38** fighters with the ability to accompany the bombers into Germany, to provoke the Luftwaffe to ever-increasing reaction and to cut the German fighter force to pieces. From the historic first **Mustang**-covered raid on Kiel on 13th December, 1943, the campaign's issue was not in doubt.

At about the same time, RAF Bomber Command, led since 22nd February, 1942, by the redoubtable

Air Marshal Harris, was taking its place in the combined bomber offensive. Harris, and his deputy, Robert Saundby, were the RAF's apostles of strategic bombing, but the excellent force they led had had a protracted and difficult birth.

With aircraft, bombs and training inadequate for the purpose, the early years saw little bite from the Command's heroic efforts. Gradually, the introduction of a range of new high-capacity and specialised bombs, target-marking squadrons and accurate navigational aids transformed the scattered and ineffectual attacks of 1941 and 1942 on pin-point targets into concentrated satura-tions of industrial centres.

This commitment to the four-engined bomber did not mean that the fast, twin-engined light and medium bomber was being neglected. The ageing **Blenheims**, which gave good service up to 1942, were replaced by the **de Havilland Mosquito**, or the

American **Boston**. In company with American Groups which later formed the Ninth Air Force, they undertook a steadily-increasing series of attacks on ports, airfields, factories and communications in occupied Europe and Germany.

This pattern of complementary strategic and tactical bombing, of which the European theatre was an example, was repeated all over the world on every battlefront.

As US forces crept, island by island, towards Japan, each new base brought more enemy territory under attack – in particular the harbours and shipping upon which the Japanese relied for mobility, as the Germans did on the European railway system.

In distinction from the specialised heavies, these medium and light twins began to diversify widely. Tough and fast, they began to evolve into the first true multi-rôle combat aircraft. The **Mosquito**, introduced in September 1941, was a light bomber almost too fast to be intercepted and as such became a constant problem to the Germans. Reconnaissance and powerfully-armed fighter versions enjoyed similar advantages and, as with the **Bristol Beaufighter**, the addition of radar made it a formidable night fighter.

The **Beaufighter** was designed in 1938 as a long-range escort fighter and first reached squadrons in September, 1940. By this time German as well as British bombers were already converting to night operations and the **Beau** first saw employment as a defensive night fighter. In the Middle East it was used in its designed rôle as a long range fighter and later it became the mainstay of Coastal Command's offensive, carrying bombs, rockets or a torpedo with equal facility and success.

In Germany, a similar versatility marked the career of the **Junkers Ju 88**. Conceived as either a conventional or dive bomber, its excellent performance and adaptability made it the Luftwaffe's multi-purpose aircraft.

Starting its career with an attack on HMS Ark Royal on 26th September, 1939, it was by the end of the war involved in day and night fighting, torpedo attacks and reconnaissance.

Unable to fulfil its designed destroyer rôle because of poor performance, the **Messerschmitt Bf 110** had a successful career as a night fighter. Fitted with the FuG 220b Lichtenstein SN-2 radar set (*top*) it enabled top German night fighter aces to score heavily against RAF bomber streams.

The **Douglas A-20 Boston** (*bottom*) was one of the most famous Allied light bombers. The 15th Bombardment Squadron, USAF, were first to receive the type early in 1942 in England and 11 RAF squadrons were also equipped with it. The box formations of 18 **Bostons** on daily bombing strikes became famous in the Middle East.

The First Jets

Four early jet fighters. (*Top*) the experimental **Heinkel He 178 VI**, the first jet to fly, which was a test bed for the Heinkel HeS 3 turbojet engine. The British **Gloster G.40**, often referred to by its specification number, E.28/39, fulfilled a similar function for the Whittle-designed Power Jets W.1 engine. The sinister and potentially deadly twin jet **Messerschmitt Me 262** caused heavy casualties among Allied bombers during its operational career, which began in April, 1944. Serviceability was not always high, however, and it became possible to trap it with piston-engined fighters. The **Gloster Meteor** (*bottom*), is seen in the colours of No. 616 Squadron, the first to receive it in July, 1944.

The First World War had given birth to no fundamentally new concepts in military flying and equipment and technique continued unchanged in form for twenty years. When the Second World War ended, however, its latter days had seen the birth of a form of propulsion that was to take flying into a new age and radically change the direction and pace of research and development.

The jet engine, like many other discoveries of wide application, appeared almost simultaneously in more than one country. Whittle in England and von Ohain in Germany were both working on jet propulsion in the mid-1930s, and both successfully bench-tested engines in 1937 – Whittle the first by a few months.

The Germans were the first to fly, the experimental **Heinkel He 178 VI** taking the air on 27th August, 1939, followed by the first jet fighter – and first twin engined jet – in April, 1941. This, the **He 280**, did not go into

service, and the honour, if such it be, of being the first operational jet fighter in the world goes to Messerschmitt's **Me 262**. First flown in July, 1942, production aircraft reached the Erprobungskommando-262, an operational evaluation unit, in June, 1944. Despite various stories of political interference, this was for the time a reasonably rapid introduction to service – although it seems certain that the higher command of the Luftwaffe were unaccountably uninterested in the new weapon.

A fast bomber version was developed (replacing the **Ju 88**), and Kampfgeschwader 51 began to be equipped with it in August, 1944, but it was as an interceptor that the **Me 262** won its greatest fame. Jagdgeschwader 7, the first fully jet unit, claimed 427 kills between November, 1944 and the end of hostilities, a total that included more than 300 four-engined bombers. Another élite unit, raised by General Galland, JV 44, exploiting the aircraft's armament of 24 air-to-air rockets and four 30mm cannon, shot down 50 bombers in an operational career of only one month.

Although six more Geschwader were forming as fighter-bomber units, none was completed in time to achieve any operational success before the collapse of the Luftwaffe with the rest of the German forces.

British development of jet aircraft was slightly slower, the first flight of the **Gloster E.28/39** (the first British jet aircraft) taking place on 15th May, 1941, but with the first operational fighter flying in March, 1943, the RAF was in action almost as soon as the Germans.

No 616 Squadron began receiving twin-engined **Gloster**

Meteor Is in July and August, 1944, going into action against flying bombs – a duty for which, with the fast piston-engined **Hawker Tempest**, they were very suitable.

A flight of 616 Squadron was sent to Evère aerodrome, Brussels, in January, 1945, when it became apparent that, despite some success with **P-51** and **P-47** against the new threat, jet combat with the Me 262 was inevitable if the war continued.

Although the squadron saw action from April and was joined by a second Meteor Squadron, No 504, flying **Meteor III**s, no jet combats took place.

The Specialists

Inadequate as an interceptor, the **Hawker Typhoon** became a devastating interdiction fighter-bomber with 2000lb of bombs or 16 60-lb rockets, in north-west Europe in 1944.

The origins of the fighter-bomber go back to 1918, to a time when the great German March offensive was harassed and worried by British single-seaters armed with nothing more powerful than two Vickers guns and a few 20-pound bombs.

The Germans themselves revived the practice in Spain with the **Heinkel He 51** biplanes that were replaced as fighters by the **Bf 109**. The experiment was a success and it was not surprising to find trials undertaken, in the summer of 1940, with a 500lb bomb under a **Bf 109**.

Towards the end of the Battle of Britain, the weight of bombs being dropped was increased by Jagdbomberstaffeln in the Jagdgeschwadern. The **Fw 190** was similarly equipped from the Spring of 1942, carrying a 1000lb bomb or its equivalent in smaller missiles.

Britain was not slow to follow suit. The **Hurricane**, an able weight-carrier, took on a new lease of life with two 250-pound bombs (later increased to 500 pounds), adding punch to Malta's air force in September, 1941.

Hurricane bombers of No 607 Squadron had replaced the light bombers of No 2 Group in the anti-shipping strikes known as "Channel Stop" in October, 1941. Three other **Hurricane** squadrons were added and in late 1942 the **Hawker Typhoon** arrived.

Disappointing as a pure fighter, the **Typhoon** found its place as the Hurricane's successor in ground attack work. Equipped with the devastating 60-pound rocket, **Typhoons** played a vital part in the invasion of Europe, initially by knocking out coastal radar stations and later by wholesale destruction of German armour.

The rocket became a most useful weapon in quite a different armoury, when Coastal Command began to receive the aircraft to use it in their ceaseless war on the U-boat.

This relentless submarine warfare epitomises the work of the Command. Starting the war with 12 squadrons of **Ansons** for Coastal patrol and only three squadrons of the long range **Sunderland**, not to mention other units equipped with obsolete biplanes, Coastal were always short of modern aircraft because other Commands had always prior claims. But they managed to do their share in containing the U-boat through the determination and gallantry of the crews.

Hudsons from America replaced the Ansons and more Sunderland squadrons were formed. When the **Whitley** became obsolete for bomber operations, it was "handed down" to Coastal, and **Wellingtons** appeared when there were enough to go round.

The **Hudson**, developed from a **Lockheed** airliner, was a most useful medium range anti-submarine aircraft – so useful that one from 269 Squadron made history on 27th August, 1941, by capturing U-570 (which later became HMS Graph). So seriously did they take their duties that one Hudson squadron bombed a ski-resort hotel at Finse, Norway, which was used as a rest centre for U-boat crews.

The comparatively short range of these various aircraft left two great gaps in the aircraft cover of the convoy routes, in mid-Atlantic and in the Bay of Biscay. Starting in 1942, long-range aircraft (assisted by close cover provided for convoys by the small escort carriers then entering service) gradually began to fill them in. There was a priceless acquisition of three USAAF **Liberator** squadrons, replaced by US Navy units when the US Army took back its **Liberators** for the North African landings. First one, then two **Fortress** squadrons started work from the Azores. The very long range **Catalinas** operated from both sides of the Atlantic, with RAF, RCAF and American squadrons.

By the end of 1942, there were few U-boat successes in the Eastern Atlantic, and Canadian

Cansos (amphibian **Catalinas**) soon closed up the Western end. The central gap still existed at this time and the last great U-boat offensive started in the Spring of 1943. In May, there were 202 sightings and 128 attacks from British bases alone.

The introduction of rockets and new anti-submarine bombs that could be dropped from higher altitude than depth-charges were a help, but at this stage Coastal Command crews only subdued the submarine by accepting very heavy losses in pressing home attacks.

But the battle was being won, in spite of such advantages to the enemy as the introduction in February, 1944, of the snorkel, a breathing device permitting underwater running on main Diesel engines.

This gave higher underwater speeds and ranges and meant that submarines did not have to surface to recharge their batteries for the electric motors previously used for underwater running.

In March, 1944, there were only four ship sinkings in the North convoy area. Even the appearance of the 16-knot-underwater Type XXI U-boat in April was too late to affect the issue.

By 1944, U-boats were forced to run on the surface to their operational areas, to save time and escape Allied minefields. When attacked, they shot it out with their heavy anti-aircraft armament.

The Carrier War

The British had received a sharp lesson in the realities of air war at the time of the Norwegian campaign, losing two aircraft carriers by working them uncovered too close to the enemy. For most of the rest of the war, the Royal Navy, preoccupied with convoy defence and other conventional operations, employed carriers largely to provide fleet air cover or to extend the range of battleships' guns.

It fell to the Americans to develop independent carrier strategy in the enormous Pacific theatre.

As far back as 1929, the US Navy had experimented with the use of the aircraft carrier as an independent weapon of offense. Circumstances were now to force them into making it the main armament of their fleet.

The attack on Pearl Harbor on 7th December, 1941, sank or damaged eight battleships, three cruisers and a number of other ships, putting the "conventional" Pacific fleet out of action. It also destroyed over 300 precious aircraft. (The US Navy, like the Army, was short of modern front-line types.)

It did not destroy the three big aircraft carriers of the Pacific Fleet. USS Saratoga was State-side, Lexington and Enterprise at sea. On that fact hung the issue of the war.

After the attack, they were joined by Hornet and Yorktown from the Atlantic and the Americans had an all-carrier fleet.

With it, they struck back. In early raids they learned that carriers could be defended by their own weapons and began operating unified air groups from two ships under one command.

On 17th April, 1942, General Doolittle's famous **B-25** raid reached Japan from the Hornet.

Early in May, the Japanese moved towards Port Moresby and the sensitive area of northern Australia, where General MacArthur was trying to build up Allied strength. The resultant American counterattack developed into the battle of the Coral Sea, with two powerful carrier forces fighting it out over the horizon in the first all-carrier engagement in the world.

Immediate honours were even. Each side had a carrier sunk, the Americans losing the great 33,000-ton Lexington. But the two Japanese fleet carriers were hit so hard that they were not available at Midway and when the invasion force returned later to Port Moresby, it had been reinforced and was held.

It was evident to the Japanese that they must destroy the American fleet and to draw them into battle Admiral Yamamoto struck at Midway Island with an invasion force protected by six carriers and a powerful force of battleships and cruisers. To this Admiral Nimitz could oppose three carriers and nine cruisers. Lacking the ability to cover them, he left his few battleships out of the action.

The battle of Midway has acquired the title of "turning point of the Pacific war", and indeed it was just that. Sighted

700 miles from Midway on 3rd June, 1942, the Japanese were attacked by Army **B-17**s, without success. For five hours, from 05.34 on the 4th, Marine fighters from Midway and Navy and Army bombers and torpedoplanes tried in vain to reach their opponents. Heavy anti-aircraft fire and Japanese fighters cut down over 80 and no hits were scored.

At 10.24, while the Japanese guns and fighters were occupied by the gallant attacks of obsolete **Devastator** torpedo bombers at sea level, the **Dauntless** dive bomber groups from Enterprise and Yorktown struck from clear skies at 17,000 feet. Their 1000-pound bombs, released at 2500 feet, so shattered three of the four Japanese fleet carriers that they could neither launch nor recover aircraft and within 24 hours all had sunk. The fourth, unscathed, launched a strike that crippled Yorktown; two days later the American carrier was sunk by a submarine.

The Americans lost, besides the Yorktown, 132 aircraft, mostly in the futile preliminary attacks. The Japanese lost four big carriers (Hiryu, the last survivor, was caught by dive bombers from Enterprise), two cruisers and 234 aircraft. Among the 2500 officers and men who died, she lost the core of her experienced carrier striking force.

From all this savage fighting the pre-war **Douglas Dauntless** dive bomber emerged as one of the great aircraft of the war. The torpedo-carrying **Devastator** was quite unable to survive, and was replaced by the **Grumman Avenger** in 1943. In the same year the Grumman **F4F Wildcat**, barely a match for the Japanese **Zero**, was succeeded by the **F6F Hellcat** and the **Vought Corsair**. The Japanese, in the years of bitter fighting that lay ahead, never succeeded in matching this pair of fast, tough, hard-hitting carrier fighters, and American naval air power became a major factor in securing the chain of island bases that led to Japan.

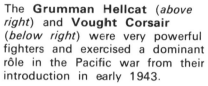

The **Grumman Avenger** (*left*) came into service in 1942 with the US Navy, a very effective weapon to replace the vulnerable **Devastator**.

The **Grumman Hellcat** (*above right*) and **Vought Corsair** (*below right*) were very powerful fighters and exercised a dominant rôle in the Pacific war from their introduction in early 1943.

Escort or "Woolworth" carriers, introduced for convoy escort in the second half of the war, and carrying 15 to 25 aircraft, were extremely effective. Nearly 130 were built.

The Big One

The **B-29** bomber from Boeing that formed the basis of Strategic Air Command. 88 were delivered to the RAF in 1950 to help bridge the gap until the V-bombers were ready.

When Colonel Lindbergh came home after his 1939 European tour, his report on the impressive growth of Nazi air power had led to his joining the Board headed by Brigadier General W. G. Kilner examining future requirements for the Army Air Corps. The Kilner Report, issued at the end of June, recommended, among other projects, the development of long-range bombers, and approval for contract studies was received by the Air Corps in December.

Under pressure of events in Europe, US ideas on national defence were changing rapidly. The Air Corps had been authorised by Congress to raise its strength to 5500 aircraft in April, 1939, and under this authority procured the first funds for what became the Hemisphere Defence project – a bomber to carry 2000 pounds of bombs 5000 miles.

The definite result of this emerged eighteen months later with a contract for two prototypes of Boeing's Model 345, the **XB-29**, and a full-size mock-up, at a cost of $3,615,095. Two hundred and fifty were ordered "off the board" in May, 1941, an order promptly doubled after Pearl Harbor and increased to 1600 two months later.

A remarkably advanced project, with a highly sophisticated, remote-control gun system, centralised and computer-controlled, the **B-29** carried eleven 0·50 inch machineguns in five turrets (some early aircraft had a 20mm in the tail, some later ones two additional 0·50s in the front turret) and had a maximum bomb load of 20,000 pounds. Maximum range was between 3250 and 4100 miles. The bomber spanned 141 feet 3 inches and carried a crew of ten.

Throughout its career the **B-29** was plagued by engine troubles, and of the 267 aircraft lost through non-combat operational causes, probably most were from power-plant failures.

The strategic possibilities of this bomber were recognised early and it was reserved exclusively for attacks on the Japanese homeland and neighbouring territories, hitherto well out of range of normal aircraft. The very scope and capability of this new weapon, as well as the fact that it had to be preserved from attempts by theatre commanders to obtain control of it, dictated

the creation of an entirely new Air Force, the 20th, to operate the **B-29**s, of which eventually there were six Bombardment Wings, each of some 180 aircraft, and a Wing of a photo-reconnaissance version, the **F-13**.

Initially, because of the distances involved, the aircraft would be based in India and operate from forward airfields in China.

Operations from China were not satisfactory. Far too much time had to be spent humping fuel and stores out of India in the bombers and there were other problems. Nevertheless the **Superfortresses** flew 49 missions, dropping 11,477 tons of bombs. The capture of the Marianas, however, during July and August, 1944, gave the Americans the bases they needed at a reasonable range from Japan, and following a series of shake-down attacks in October and November, 20th Air Force settled into high altitude precision bombing of industrial targets. These, unfortunately, were not effective and in February, 1945, after some argument at top level, the **B-29**s began a devastating series of fire raids on Japan.

The series was never completed. At 0915 hours on 6th August, 1945, a **B-29** of 509th Bombardment Wing dropped the first of the two atomic bombs delivered in anger and the war came to an end with Japan's surrender on 2nd September.

The famous **North American Harvard** trainer (*top*) was the RAF's first American aircraft. On the **Tiger Moth** (*top centre*) almost every British or Commonwealth pilot in the Second World War was trained. The **Bucker Jungmeister** (*lower centre*) was a German advanced trainer of the 1930s that had become an aerobatic connoisseur's item in the 1970s. The big, amiable **Stearman** primary trainer, with a variety of motors, was the principal trainer of all the US services. A **PT-17** to the Army, the one shown (*bottom*) is a US Navy **N2S-2**.

To most American servicemen, the big **Douglas C-54** meant the start of the journey home at the end of their war. The first of the four-engined transports, it helped to keep casualty rates low by fast evacuation to base hospitals and was a factor in the preparation of the public mind to accept post-war air travel.

The Trainers and Transports

The development of air power and air operations during the Second World War had brought into prominence two neglected aspects of its application: training and transport.

Both Britain and the United States, faced with the sudden flood of recruits for aircrew duties, set up specialised training programmes. The problem was not simply that of administering and training these very large numbers of recruits, but of maintaining a balanced flow and reservoir of skilled manpower in the face of shifting operational requirements and competition from the other Services and industry.

The Empire Air Training Scheme of December, 1939, provided for ample training facilities outside an embattled and crowded Britain and the formation of Flying Training and later Technical Training Commands of the Royal Air Force ensured proper control of aircrew production.

The problem of meeting fluctuating demands from operational units was met by the formation, in 1940, of Operational Training Units, where aircrew became proficient on operational types, drew experience from instructors drawn from operational units and acted as a reservoir to absorb any sudden demand for replacements. Upon occasion, crews from OTUs serving Bomber Command (who made the most use of the system) took part in operations, notably in bolstering Operation Millenium, the 1000-bomber raid series.

In the United States, similar problems brought similar answers, with training under the specialised care of First, Second and Fourth Air Forces and OTUs introduced early in 1942 – these units having the additional task of supervising the training of newly-created squadrons in the swiftly-expanding Army Air Forces.

Transport flying was an extraordinarily neglected branch of the Royal Air Force. The "bomber-transports" such as the **Vernon** and **Bombay** of prewar years were – apart from their poor performance – thought of simply as transports for troops (a legacy of the colonial war policies and practices of British administration). When, during the war, Transport Command was formed, its primary duties were indicated by naming its two major units "Ferry Groups". Although a number of civil airliners was impressed at the outbreak of war, these were used mostly for military versions of their peacetime occupation. Not until the later stages of the war, and then primarily in the remoter theatres, was air power used to supply its own needs. In the same way, the evacuation of casualties by air was developed by force of the lack of any alternative.

The Americans, with a better-developed sense of the uses of air transport, developed their supply systems more rapidly and more thoroughly. One aspect of transport work that helped to bring it into prominence was the increasing number of crews and aircraft required for airborne operations to bring troops by air into battle.

From their pre-eminent position in this field, as will be seen, the Americans were to draw a considerable advantage in peacetime.

Europe – The Postwar Scene

When the Second World War ended, plans for post-war civil aviation began to be put into operation in Britain, France and the USA. In all three countries, pre-war or wartime aircraft formed the basis of the new commercial air fleets, designed to operate over routes almost identical to those run before the war.

France was unfortunate in these early developments. Her industry, crippled by the years of occupation and the results of Allied bombing, had nevertheless succeeded in continuing some civil work, but neither the SNCASE **SE 161 Languedoc** nor the **SE 2010 Armagnac** was very successful. The first, developed from a 1936 requirement through the 1939 **Bloch 161**, was plagued with mechanical troubles, although Air France used 40 of the 100 built on European and African routes from 1947 to 1954. The **Armagnac**, on which great hopes were placed, grew from wartime studies for a France-Africa or Atlantic airliner. It was designed for sleeper configuration, with a very deep fuselage to take three tiers of bunks, but by the time it first flew on 2nd April, 1949, this concept of air travel was dead.

Economic use of the aircraft for normal passenger work being unlikely, Air France did not take delivery and seven of the nine built spent much of their life in transport duties with the SAGETA Company during the Indo-Chinese war.

In Britain, the Brabazon Committee in 1943 had formulated a series of Specifications for airliners, to cover projected post-war needs. Although the Committee underestimated the actual volume of North Atlantic traffic (as, indeed, did the Americans) and the aircraft built to *Type I*, the **Bristol Brabazon** was, for various reasons, a gigantic and costly failure, most of the other Specifications bore successful fruit. *Type IIA* resulted in the **Airspeed Ambassador**, originally intended as a **DC-3** replacement; of the 23 built, all but five were still flying almost twenty years after the type's first flight. *Type IIB* covered the **Vickers Viscount**. *Type III* was an Avro project, the **690** or **Avro XXII** (for which four-jet aircraft the ill-fated Tudor series were to have served as interim types). *Type IV* was the **de Havilland Comet** and *Type VA* the **Miles Marathon**.

Type VB gave rise to the **de Havilland Dove** of 1945, an extremely successful feeder-liner and charter aircraft of which 527 were eventually built in eight marks. Many examples of the **Dove**, which first entered airline service with Central African Airways in December, 1946, were still flying with various owners in 1973 and the type gained the distinction of being the first British aircraft to sell competitively in some numbers in America.

Prior to the availability of some of the more advanced aircraft built to Brabazon Specifications, the British Government encouraged a number of interim types. One of these was the **Avro Lancastrian**, a converted Lancaster bomber that commenced trans-Atlantic passenger flights for Trans-Canada Air Lines in the summer of 1943. A civil airliner based on the Lancaster but with a completely new fuselage, the **Avro York**, was designed during the war. Between 1943 and 1948, 256 were built, the majority for RAF transport squadrons, but BOAC received 30. Seating up to 24 passengers and cruising at between 210 and 230mph, the **York** was a useful aircraft for its day. Continuing dollar shortages extended that day until 1957, for **York**s went on to give useful service with smaller operators, tour and charter firms and freight lines, inaugurating a "hand-me-down" life-cycle for airliners that persists to this day.

Another successful British airliner that came into being as a Government-commissioned interim type was the **Vickers Viking**, a twin-engined all-metal short-range aircraft seating 24–36 passengers, whose origins are sufficiently obvious in its resemblance to the Wellington bomber – it bore the same relationship to it as did the **York** to the Lancaster.

It entered service with the newly-formed British European Airways Corporation in August, 1946, and proved a popular aircraft with this and other airlines, being significantly faster than the **DC-3**, of which large numbers were available as war-surplus stock. 163 were built, with 263 of a military version, the **Valetta**, which served the RAF for 11 years. Another military Viking, the crew-trainer **Varsity**, celebrated its twenty-first birthday with the RAF in 1970.

In 1939, there had been three promising British trans-Atlantic aircraft projects in design or mock-up stage. None of these was proceeded with, bomber and fighter production absorbing the whole wartime effort, and as a result, the lead that the United States was already beginning to establish in this field in 1939 with the **Boeing 314** and **307**, was to become unassailable in the decade following the war.

These British airliners of the immediate post-war period are the **Vickers Viking** of British European Air Services (BEA) (*left*), the **Avro York** of British Overseas Airways Corporation (BOAC) (*centre*) and the **Avro Lancastrian** of British South American Airways Ltd (BSAA). BOAC took over from Imperial Airways and British Airways on 1st April, 1940. It ran civil services throughout the war and used the **York** on post-war Empire routes. The British European Airways service of BOAC was formed in July, 1945, taking over routes in Europe served by 110 Wing, RAF. BSAA, formed independently in 1946 by a number of shipping companies, became a national Corporation the same year. Following aircraft problems arising from the loss of Star Tiger and Star Ariel, two of their **Avro Tudors**, BSAA was merged with BOAC in 1948.

The first true British post-war airliner was the **de Havilland Dove** (*below right*) shown in the colours of the Brazilian Ministry of Public Works. A popular aircraft, it achieved wide overseas sales.

The New Generation

The pattern of post-war airline development in the USA was very much a continuation of the pre-war picture, with an added stimulus from the greatly increased awareness of air travel among the American population and a magnificent bonus in the shape of large numbers of surplus **DC-3** military transports and **Douglas C-54**s.

The "Big Four" and their smaller brethren returned to civil work with the experience of some four years of very intense activity on the domestic routes, which was continued by a post-war boom.

The Douglas **DC-4**, the military C-54, flew for the first time on 14th February, 1942. It had been developed in 1940 as a result of consultations with five American airlines and following Pearl Harbor the production line, consisting at that time of an initial batch of 24 aircraft, was taken over by the Army. 1154 were built and with them the military transport organisation built up a unique experience of regular long-distance schedules.

With one notable exception, the major airlines all put their future in the hands of the **DC-4**, following the first civil service introduced by Western on 18th January, 1946.

The exception was Howard Hughes' airline, Transcontinental & Western Air, which backed the magnificent **Lockheed Constellation**.

Like the **DC-4**, the **Constellation** production line had been requisitioned, but only 22 were built before the end of hostilities spelled the end of the contract.

The "Connie", as it later became affectionately known, set off a fierce struggle for technical supremacy on the air routes, in particular on the transcontinental and trans-Atlantic runs. Competition was the lifeblood of American airline development policy and in these great arteries the pace was accelerating.

Sixty-five miles an hour faster than the **DC-4** and of striking good looks, it carried 16 more passengers and – most important of all – was pressurised, which the **DC-4** was not.

TWA put the **Constellation** into service on the New York-Los Angeles service on 1st March, 1946. It was not until a year later that American and United countered with the first of the Douglas **DC-6**s.

The "Dash Six" was comparable to the early **Constellations**, carrying 50 first class or 68 tourist passengers at 280mph. By 1951, via a more powerful version, the **DC-6A**, Douglas were offering the very successful **DC-6B**, stretched still further to accommodate up to 102 high-density seats, and cruising at the same speed as the much lighter **DC-6**. It was the best of all the Douglas transports, including the later **DC-7** series, largely because it turned out to be extremely economical to run.

Lockheed were not idle while this was going on, having designed the **L.1049 Super-Constellation**, stretched and increased in power, in 1951. Slower than the **DC-6B**, however, it did not sell as well as the Douglas, though offering equally low seat-mile costs, and Lockheed temporarily lost the advantage in the airline "war".

In 1953, however, they brought out the **L.1049C**, which had been developed at the expense of the US Navy, to whom the firm had sold the military version. TWA reaped an immediate benefit when this aircraft appeared on the trans-continental route, utilising its greater range by introducing the first non-stop service from Los Angeles to New York, in an unprecedented 8 hours.

Much of the success of the **L.1049C** was due to its power plants, 3250hp Wright Turbo-Cyclone compound engines. These motors also powered the Douglas counter to the **Super-Constellation**, the **DC-7** series, introduced in 1953. To this, Lockheed replied with the G-series **L.1049**, the ultimate development in this particular duel, and which enjoyed a reputation equal to that of the original "Connie".

The turbo-compound engine, which represented the ultimate development in piston engine design, in the hope of challenging the new British propeller-gas turbine, provided rather too much power for the DC "Seven Seas" (-7C) and **Super-Constellation** and both Douglas and Lockheed redesigned their wings to put the engines further from the cabin and reduce the considerable noise and vibration.

It was equally the **Constellation** that began to dominate the prized North Atlantic route and here PanAmerican come into the picture. Without domestic mileage but having built up a monopoly of overseas operations, PanAm were fighting hard to retain that position after the war. They did not entirely succeed and eventually the US Government principle of competition allowed other carriers to intervene. This boiled down to a fight between PanAmerican and TWA on the Atlantic sector.

The weapons – the Douglases and the Lockheeds – were the same, but early in the game, to counter the original **L.049 Constellation**, PanAm introduced the **Boeing Stratocruiser**.

Boeing had abandoned airliner design when they became totally involved in bombers, but came back with a pressurised, two-deck civil fuselage on a **B-29** wing – having first amortised their research and development costs with a military order for 77 transports and 811 tankers. A number of US airlines ordered the **Stratocruiser**, whose standard of luxury made it very popular with passengers, and it served on trans-Continental, as well as Atlantic and Pacific routes.

Three great piston-engined airliners that established the USA in a leading position for building transport aircraft. The early model **Lockheed Constellation** (*left*) carried up to 69 passengers at 270mph on four 2200-hp Wright R-3350s. Pan American, in whose colours it is shown, were also the largest users of the **Boeing Stratocruiser** shown above it. Douglas's **DC-6**, here in the colours of Scandinavian Airlines System and shown about to inaugurate their famous Over the Pole service, used the 2500-hp Pratt and Whitney R-2800 engine.

British development of the propeller turbine gave aircraft like the **Vickers Viscount** an edge on the competitive airline market, and it was still in service in 1973, 23 years after flying its first scheduled service.

The Bold Decision

The lead gained by the United States in airliner construction through their possession of the resources and the market to nourish the product of their skill in design, would obviously need a tremendous effort to overtake – if it could be done at all.

The design staff at de Havilland, with a history of successful fast aircraft and early experience in jet engines which they had built themselves, felt they could make this effort, and design studies began after they had persuaded the 1943 Brabazon Committee to draft a specification for a jet airliner. The Committee, who did not, it seems, share de Havilland's optimism, proposed a high-speed mailplane, to cross the Atlantic with six passengers and 5000 pounds of mail.

As "D.H." studied jet operations more deeply, their plans grew in stature until the **Comet I** flew for the first time in 1949. It was a giant step into the darkness of very fast, very high altitude commercial flying intended to put Britain five years in the lead. It was, unfortunately, too great a step. Structural and aerodynamic deficiencies led to the **Comet**'s withdrawal after a series of disasters and when the **Comet 4** finally made a successful appearance, it was only weeks ahead of the **Boeing 707**.

A much happier story was that of the short-range **Vickers Viscount**. Developed from operational experience with the **Viking**, it was the first gas-turbine propellor airliner in the world. It held this lead for four years, when the long range **Bristol Britannia** appeared and its economy, speed and quiet, vibrationless travel gave it enormous success.

The prototype **de Havilland Comet I**, seen here preparing for flight, set out to solve the problems of very high-speed, very high-altitude flying on commercial routes. The design overreached itself and by the time the problems had been solved, **Boeing** had caught up.

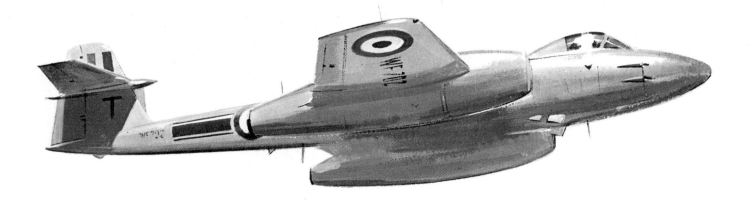

The Jet War

The Korean war opened on 25th June, 1950, when Communist forces from North Korea attacked across the 38th parallel. The Korean People's Armed Forces Air Corps in the North, consisting of some 130-odd **Yak-9** fighters, **Il-10** attack aircraft and **Yak-18** trainers, had little to fear from the Republic of Korea Air Force with **Piper L-4** liaison aircraft and North American **T-6** trainers. In fact, the first blow destroyed a **C-54** of the American 5th Air Force on the ground at Kimpo. **F-82** long-range fighters operating from Japan to cover transport aircraft evacuating American dependents shot down three **Yak-9s** two days later.

American troops, initially only lightly armed, were called in to defend the port of Pusan, joined shortly by UN contingents from Britain, Australia and Turkey that were to include an **F-51**-equipped Wing of the RAAF. The US Far Eastern Air Force, created to provide air support, began a steadily mounting campaign of close support and interdiction with **F-80** jet fighters and piston-engined **B-26** bombers, while two groups of **B-29s** opened a series of constant attacks on North Korean airfields and supply and communications centres.

The destruction was claimed of 110 North Korean aircraft and the army investing Pusan was virtually destroyed. When UN troops under General MacArthur attacked northwards they were preceded by massive air strikes and received a major portion of their supplies by air.

The sweep into North Korea and the destruction of the enemy's armed forces brought the Chinese into the battle, Chinese **MiG-15** fighters appearing on 1st November and the first jet air battle in history occurring with **F-80s** seven days later. Meanwhile, reinforced **B-29** squadrons bombed and burned strategic targets in an attempt to discourage the Chinese.

In this they failed, and UN troops were pushed back, under a very effective fighter and bomber screen, to South Korea. The **F-80** and **F-51** were no match for the **MiG-15**, but in mid-December reinforcements of **F-86** and **F-84** units arrived. The front stabilised in the winter of 1950–1951, and FEAF concentrated on destroying Communist airfields and supplies to frustrate the build-up for a Chinese spring offensive. Large air battles built up in this period in "MiG Alley". The expected offensive in April and May was largely defeated by air power.

Throughout the uneasy summer, the Chinese fought to build up supplies, while Strategic Air Command **B-29s** and fighter bombers from 5th Air Force savaged the Korean rail system. The Chinese, in an attempt to achieve air superiority, which they recognised to be vital to success, built up a force of an estimated 1255 aircraft, including 525 **MiG-15s**. The 105 **F-86s** facing them were reinforced in February 1952 by a further Wing and the Chinese bid failed.

The railway campaign, only partially successful, was called off in May, 1952, and replaced by an "air pressure" campaign designed to destroy the enemy's fighter force and a series of targets vital to his war-making capacity.

The Chinese responded savagely and in heavy air battles through the next year the Americans, reinforced by superior **F-86F** fighter bombers, took a heavy toll of **MiGs** – 75 for no loss in June, 1953. A campaign of attacks on communications emphasised US domination of Korean air, which helped to defeat the last Communist ground offensive in June–July and the final operations were the wholesale destruction of **MiG-15s** on the surviving airfields of North Korea.

The **North American Sabre** (*right*) was undoubtedly the most famous of all US jet fighters. Conceived as a military version of the straight wing Navy **NA Fury FJ-1**, the availability of data from Germany on swept wings made it possible to revise the design to a more advanced level. The **Sabre** wings, with their typically German leading-edge slats, were basically the same as those intended for a swept-wing version of the **Me 262**. The **F-86A** version of the **Sabre**, armed with six 0·50 machine guns, went into action in Korea to replace the **Mustangs** and **Shooting Stars**, the 4th Fighter Interception Wing recording the first all-jet air battle in history on 17th December, 1950.

The only British jet to see action in Korea was the **Gloster Meteor**. The Mk 8 version of this twin-engined fighter, which entered RAF service in June, 1950 with 245 Squadron, was used by 77 Squadron, RAAF, following a period of Korean operations with the **P-51 Mustang**. The **Meteor** (*above*) is in the colours of 41 Squadron, RAF.

The Tough Ones

The **Hawker Hunter FGA Mk 9** (*far left*) was the last ground-attack version of this famous aircraft to serve with the RAF. The **North American F-100 Super Sabre** (*left*) set a world speed record in 1953, and the **English Electric Canberra** (*below*) held many point-to-point records.

Roughly contemporary designs, the three aircraft featured here serve as indicators of the advances in combat aircraft design during the fruitful period of the 1950s. In a way, they are the bridge between two differing technologies, two steps in the evolution of the application of military air power. They are the last of the aircraft designed for one task and adapted for others; the first, perhaps, to come really near the true multi-rôle combat aircraft that have come after them. To them was given the combination of superb aerodynamic design allied to increasingly powerful engines, but they were too early for the complex, sophisticated support of computers, attack navigation aids and weapon delivery systems that gave the later aircraft, the **Mirages**, the **Harriers**, the **Jaguars** and the **Phantoms**, an awe-inspiring versatility.

The English Electric **Canberra** was designed to a Specification written near the war's end and first flew in 1949. It was the first jet bomber in the RAF and closely paralleled in its career its illustrious predecessor the **Mosquito**. Like the Mosquito, it was fast enough to eschew armament in the bomber versions. Designed by W. E. Petter, who

was also responsible for the **Gnat**, the **Canberra B.2** entered service with Bomber Command in 1951, eventually equipping 27 squadrons, with 13 others in overseas Commands. A later version, the **B.6**, more powerful and with greater range, was the first RAF jet bomber to see action, during anti-terrorist operations in Malaysia. It later took part in the Suez landing.

With the introduction of V-bombers into Bomber Command, the **Canberras** were concentrated in the Near and Far East as a nuclear strike force. Two further versions were produced for photo-reconnaissance and the final combat version, the **B(I)8**, was an intruder in the tradition of the **Mosquito** and **Boston** and **Havoc**. The five squadrons in Germany trained for low-level nuclear attack – forerunners of the ill-fated **TSR2** and the successful **Buccaneer**, as well as conventional intruder-interdiction work.

The design team led by Sir Sidney Camm had a reputation for producing very rugged and adaptable aircraft. The Hunter was no exception. Its entry into Fighter Command was delayed by aerodynamic problems, but eventually more than 1000 were

supplied to 30 squadrons. Powerfully armed with four 30mm Aden guns and 2000 pounds of bombs, rockets or napalm, it served until replaced by the supersonic **Lightning** in 1960. A year before that, a ground attack version reached squadrons and saw 11 years of very successful service. Twenty-two years after its first flight, the **Hunter** was still in demand with foreign air forces and, like the **Canberra**, continued to sell well.

A little later in inception, the **F-100** fighter, first of the "century" series and first production fighter capable of level supersonic flight, incorporated lessons learned from the excellent **F-86 Sabre**. Only slightly bigger, but with greatly increased power (17,000lb thrust with afterburner), the **Super Sabre** entered Service in 1953 and stayed on to do valuable work in close-support missions over Vietnam. With a maximum bomb-load of 6000 pounds on its underwing pylons, and with missiles supplementing the basic armament of four 20mm cannon, it was a very versatile aircraft. It served also in Europe with tactical fighter squadrons.

In 1970, the **F-4** and **F-111** began to replace it.

The Big Stick

Entering service with 93rd Heavy Bombardment Wing of the USAF, the 185-foot-span, 480,000-lb **B-52** was the first of the strategic weapons systems, which regarded the actual aircraft as only an integrated part of the complex structure evolved to deliver blows. Main deterrent in the armoury of the USA, with its round-the-world nuclear attack capability, it was freed for tactical tasks (as was the British V-bomber force) when Intercontinental Ballistic Missiles (ICBM) became realistic weapons. In this rôle it began operating from Thailand against targets in Vietnam in 1965. **B-52G** 59-2592, nineteenth of the last batch built, is seen as Lavender Panther of the 92nd Bomb Squadron, 92nd Strategic Aerospace Wing, USAF, dumping 1000lb conventional bombs.

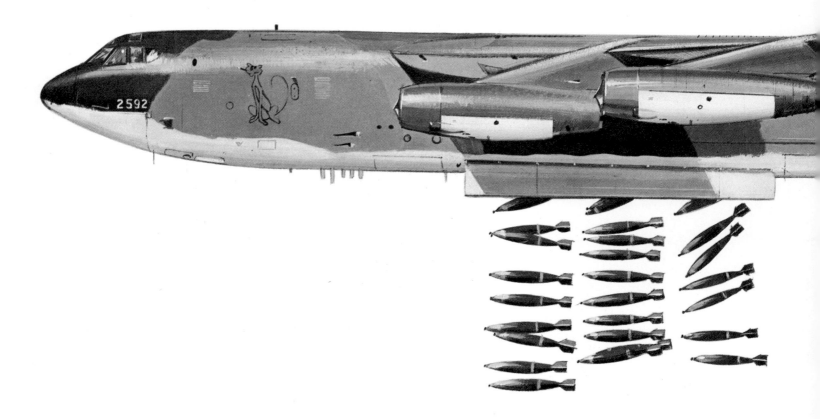

The wholesale destruction of sections of Germany and Japan by strategic bombardment had given Allied air leaders a conviction that their theories were right – that strategic bombardment was a war-winning weapon. Nowhere was this view more firmly held than in the United States, where the Bombardment Groups of the Eighth, Fifteenth and Twentieth Air Forces had finally proved their point. Large numbers of heavy bombers *could* fight their way to selected targets, destroy them, and in the process blunt the enemy's defensive fighter weapon.

Having proved the bomber to be – as had always been claimed – the offensive arm of an air force, General Arnold had no problem in principle in building the post-war American Air Force round Strategic Air Command (SAC), established in March, 1946. Of problems, its first commander, General Kenney, had in fact plenty.

On paper he commanded two Air Forces, the Eighth and Fifteenth, but demobilisation had reduced these to nine bombardment groups of **B-29**s and **B-17**s and a handful of **P-51** fighters.

It took four years to modernise and expand SAC into a force that could actually deliver the atomic bomb that only the USA then possessed. In 1948, the **B-50** began to replace the ageing **B-29**, and in 1950 the first of the mighty **B-36**s arrived. With a 10,000 mile range this six-engined, 230-foot-span 170-ton monster was the backbone of SAC until the **B-52**s came into service in 1955. With four jet engines added to boost speed over the target to 435mph and a bombload that could include two twenty-ton conventional bombs, it was a formidable weapon.

The acquisition of the **B-36**s sparked off a bitter inter-service fight over global strategy. The Navy wanted to see their "supercarriers" built with the money used to buy the big bomber. The carriers were cancelled and SAC won the day, helped by the events of the Korean war, where SAC **B-29**s were in action, despite massive and effective work in that theatre by carrier-based aviation.

Korea accelerated the provision of the new **B-47** jet bombers and the acquisition of overseas bases, which, combined with standard employment of in-flight refuelling, gave SAC a really global reach. The **B-52** eight-engined jet bomber came into service in 1955, relegating the **B-47** to medium bombardment duties. Two years later, SAC had 45 bombardment wings and, when the last **B-36** retired in 1959, became an all-jet force.

B-52 production ceased in October, 1963. SAC units in Thailand employed it to drop conventional bombs in Vietnam, and in the following five years the reshaping of the nuclear deterrent force brought SAC's inventory down to some 450 of the type. From 1971, 96 of these began to be modified to carry 20 Short Range Attack Missiles each, as Strategic Air Command up-dated its armoury.

In 1960, two wings of the supersonic **B-58** Hustler, the 43rd and 305th, joined SAC, serving until the aircraft was withdrawn in 1970.

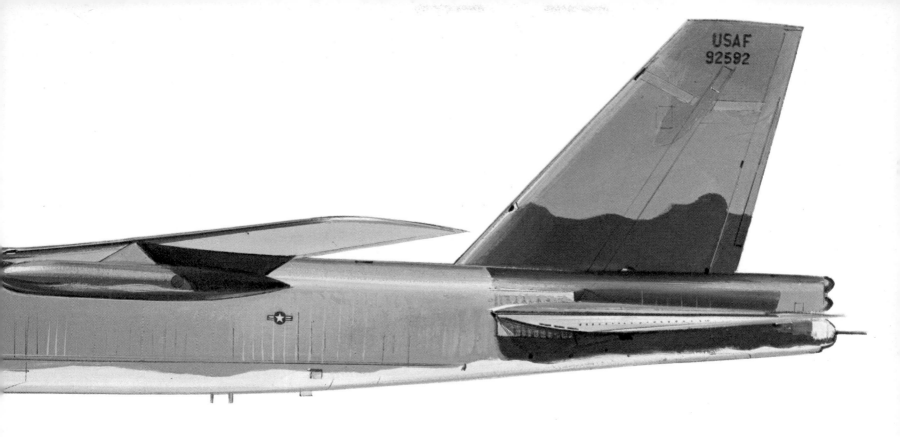

The ability of strategic bombers to range world-wide depended on an elaborate airborne refuelling service. In the picture (*below*), a **Boeing B-47**, forerunner of the **B-52**, is seen approaching the tanker's boom for a refuelling rendezvous at high altitude.

The Spy in the Sky

The story of reconnaissance from the air was the original story of the world's first air forces. Considered in 1914 to be the prime task for aircraft, its fast-growing success (particularly with the British development of aerial photography) forced counter-measures that led to the beginning of aerial warfare.

Aerial photography was brought to a fine art – again by the British – in the Second World War. The superb Williamson cameras and the development of fast, unarmed, high-altitude photo-recce variants of **Spitfire** and **Mosquito** produced tactical and strategic coverage of all Europe. Subjected to photographic interpretation, which the RAF had also brought to a high degree of excellence, it provided confirmation of bombing results and information on the enemy's efforts and defensive measures, with a minuteness of detail that seemed at the time to be almost magical. The introduction of more specialised aircraft since the war has been accompanied by better lenses, the use of colour and infra-red photography and techniques developed in many cases from the thriving business of peaceful air survey.

PR operations are by their nature unobtrusive, if they are to succeed, but the shooting-down of an American reconnaissance aircraft near Sverdlovsk in the USSR on May Day, 1960, gave a most embarrassing publicity to a certain USAF endeavour. The **Lockheed U-2** "spy-plane" employed on that flight was specially developed for espionage-reconnaissance to satisfy the Central Intelligence Agency's desire to see what the Soviet Union was doing. Its light weight (17,000lb) and great power (17,000lb thrust) gave a range of 4000 miles at 460mph. Operating at 80,000 feet, it was hoped that it would evade detection and was said to have been photographing Russia for two years before the Sverdlovsk incident. Other **U-2**s were employed in the Middle East and China.

With the development of satellites, this kind of work could be done even less obtrusively. Specialised aircraft continued to be developed, however, ranging from photo-reconnaissance versions of standard fighters such as the **Meteor**, **Mirage**, **Phantom** and **Hunter**, and bombers such as the **Canberra**, **B-47** and **B-52** to special redesigns of the Martin-built Canberra, the **RB-57**. The 64 foot span of the B-57 was increased to 106ft and later to 122ft, and more powerful engines were fitted, plus two small underwing jets. Lockheed came back into the picture with a "silent snooper", a glider-based, very quiet battlefield surveillance aircraft, the **YO-3A**, with body-heat sensors and other refinements, that was employed in Vietnam.

As the "front line" of American strategy expanded, special early warning aircraft were developed from such types as the **Super Constellation**, to carry radar coverage to greater distances. The most recent development in this field has been the USAF's Airborne Warning and Control System, fitted into a reworked **Boeing 707-320** powered by eight turbofan engines.

The availability of very long-range aircraft such as the **Super Constellation** enabled the US government to stretch radar coverage for defence purposes "around the horizon", relaying the straight-line radar waves *via* Airborne Early Warning aircraft fitted with complex electronic gear.

The latest development of this system is the Airborne Warning and Control System (AWACS) programme, intended to provide airborne control and communications centres for the airborne early warning system of Aerospace Defence Command.

The 17-man operational crew of the aircraft will provide identification, tracking and surveillance of enemy forces and control facilities for North American Air Defence (NORAD) units. The converted **Boeing 707-320B** shown is the prototype of a production order for 42 aircraft. Two of these military **EC-137D**s have been fitted with Hughes or Westinghouse downward-searching radar, housed in the big dish over the rear fuselage.

Battlefield surveillance is represented by the **Dassault Mirage IIIR** (*lower picture*). This is a photo-reconnaissance version for the French Air Force of the very successful multi-purpose fighter-ground attack **Mirage III**, latest in a line of production aircraft dating back to the first French jet fighter, the **Dassault Ouragan**. A set of five OMERA 31 cameras at different angles replaces the radar normally carried in the nose.

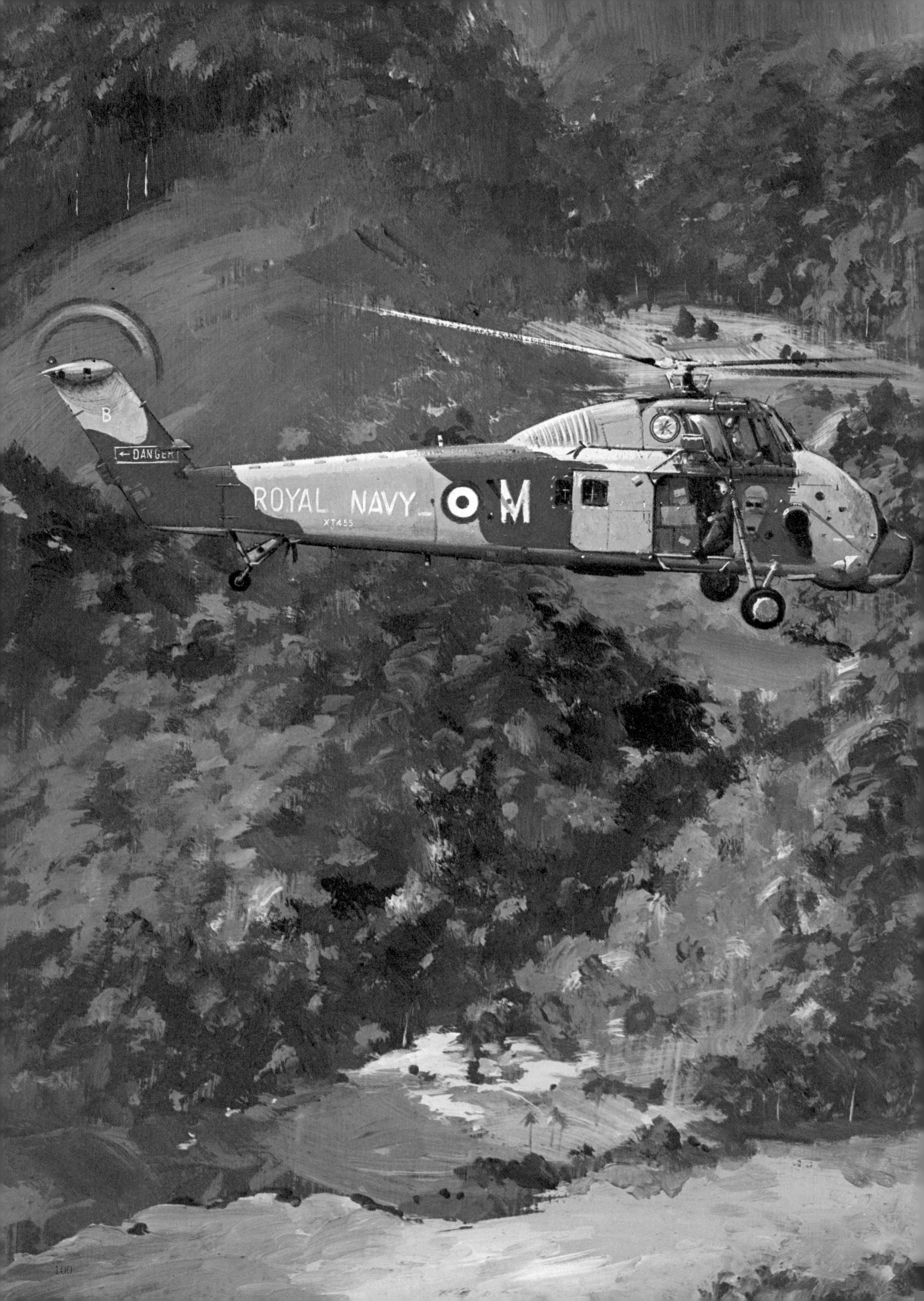
B
← DANGER
ROYAL NAVY
M
XT455

The Limited Wars

The years of the 1950s and 1960s were filled with local and bitter wars throughout the Near and Far East.

For Britain, time and patience were allies in her "brush fire" wars. In Malaya, where from 1950 to 1960 a long and eventually successful campaign was waged against Communist terrorists, tactical air strikes were manipulated by local commanders to wipe out guerrilla hide-outs after these had been located and isolated by the army. The British succeeded in isolating the guerrillas from local sympathy. Air operations were consequently in low key, conducted by **Brigands** of 45 and 84 Squadrons between 1950 and 1954, by RAF and EAAF **Lincolns** – in an unaccustomed tactical rôle and backed by 81 Squadron's photo-reconnaissance **Mosquitos**.

The first techniques of operating transport and rescue helicopters arose out of experiments in this campaign, much useful work being performed by **Sycamores** and **Dragonflies** of 199 Squadron and **Whirlwinds** of 155 Squadron of the Far East Air Force, and by RN units.

Lincolns were also employed against the Mau-Mau terrorists in Kenya, where radar-controlled bombing of hideouts began in October, 1954. **Harvards** were also employed in attack rôles, as they had been in Malaya and by the USAF in Korea. Helicopters were used in a small way by 26 Squadron in Tanganyika and the Radfan, South Arabia, and by 66 Squadron in Brunei, and also in the classic small jungle war in Borneo in 1962–66, both units operating **Belvederes**. It was during the curious and half-hearted Suez campaign, however, that British helicopter techniques came of age. The most significant air employment (apart from the **Canberra** strikes, the blooding of the new **Valiant**, first of the V-bombers, and considerable conventional fixed-wing naval support) was in the conception of the helicopter-equipped Commando carrier.

Suez apart, France was not nearly so successful in her decolonization wars. In Algeria and in Indo-China, her armed forces were hampered by political manoeuvrings and by military thinking of a previous generation of colonial soldiers. Air support, from **Thunderbolts**, **Harvards** and French-built **Vampires**, was ill-employed.

The solitary "clean", totally successful air war was, of course, fought in the course of the Six Day War between Israel and her Arab neighbours. Israel had built up her air force to about 350 front-line aircraft.

Against this the Egyptians disposed of 400 fighters and 70 twin-jet bombers.

Jordan possessed 22 **Hunters** (without enough pilots to man them all), Iraq a total of 220 aircraft, half British, half Russian.

The Israelis faced several problems in the air. Their whole country was exposed to attack from closely adjacent Arab airfields; they themselves had no long-range bombers and a fair proportion of the Arab bases were out of their reach. The attack, when it was made, was near-perfect in planning and execution. Feints had drawn much of the Egyptian air force to frontier bases. Waves of 40 Israeli aircraft at ten-minute intervals struck at breakfast time, while the Egyptian dawn patrols were refuelling. On 17 airfields, with cannon fire and bombs, they caused total chaos, destroying nearly 300 aircraft – Egypt's whole effective striking force – including all the **Tu-16**s. The whole attack was over in just under three hours.

Confusion caused by false Egyptian claims of air victory delayed entry into the air war by Jordan and Syria and enabled the Israelis to destroy the Jordanian air force and cripple the Syrian in simultaneous 20-minute attacks.

(*Far left*) A **Westland Wessex** of No 845 Squadron, Royal Navy, over the Borneo jungle. The **Boeing-Vertol Chinook** (*above right*), the US Army Corps' first VTOL transport, was widely used in Korea to carry troops and recover crashed aircraft. The **Sikorsky S-55** (*below right*), an early utility and rescue helicopter, was used by the USAF and USN in the 1950s.

The War No-one Won

The Republic F-105 Thunderchief (*above*) over the Mekong Delta was used by 388th and 355th Tactical Fighter Wings of the US Tactical Air Force in Vietnam until it was withdrawn in 1970.
Affectionately known as the "Spad", the veteran Douglas AD-1 Skyraider in 21 major sub-types, served from 1945 to 1968 and achieved undying fame in Korea and Vietnam.

The war in Vietnam opened in 1965, on much the same political pattern as that in Korea fifteen years earlier, but it dragged on for eight years.

It has been a war remarkable for the mis-use of air power in the strategic sense – using it as a bludgeon instead of as a rapier. Reduced to its basics, the problem was that neither side was equipped to damage the other mortally and had to adapt existing methods.

The French had tried to fight a 19th-century colonial war in Vietnam (Indo-China) against a modern, well-equipped force. The Americans, in their turn, deployed an enormously sophisticated military machine against an enemy who successfully defied the "air power wins wars" theory by literally going back to the jungle.

The war in the air settled into four fairly well-defined channels. Where the army was fighting along the demilitarized zone, the air force gave close support; it covered enemy rear areas in interdiction strikes; it supplied the ground forces; and far to the north, strategic bombing of Hanoi and enemy centres of supply and production were designed to weaken his will to continue.

Something went wrong with all these plans. The Americans soon discovered that close support in a jungle terrain was a very different thing from smearing the naked hills of Korea with napalm. Similarly, trying to repeat the "Operation Strangle" of Korea – the interdiction campaign against supply railroads – which had in any case achieved only limited success, they were again defeated by the jungle. Enemy supply units were broken down to the point of individuals with bicycles, moving on jungle trails at night. Complex supersonic fighter-bombers, capable of delivering appalling weights of explosive with radar-computed accuracy, were totally the wrong weapon to employ against them.

Greater and greater weights of

The Peaceful Plotters

The **Lockheed Hercules** was the first medium cargo support system aircraft for the USAF. Tough and designed to operate out of small unprepared landing fields, it has become a significant factor in increasing armed forces mobility and in pioneering new techniques. From the Arctic and Antarctic to the tropics, it has undertaken every kind of supply mission, recovered space capsules, dropped paratroops and flight-refuelled helicopters.

bombs, rockets and napalm were employed, but they merely increased the frustration. The **B-52s** of SAC were brought in to carpet the jungle with vast loads of small bombs – the ultimate in mis-employment. To offset the heavy losses incurred and to achieve better results, the Americans turned to aircraft more suited to the conflict. The unbelievable **Skyraider** (on the edge of retirement when the Korean war began), elderly **C-47s** and **C-119s** converted to heavily armed gunships, and armed helicopters were all employed to thicken up battlefield fire power. "Operation Ranch-hand", in a curious piece of inverted thinking, set out to destroy wholesale by defoliation the protective screen of the jungle.

The United States eventually became very sensitive to criticism of this costly, destructive and not very successful effort to burn down the building rather than invent a mousetrap. This showed particularly in the political control of the spasmodic and costly bombing of North Vietnam.

Most of this latter campaign was carried out by 388th and 355th Tactical Fighter Wings, armed with the powerful supersonic **F-105** Thunderchief. If the rest of the Air Force was trying to fight a primitive war, the "Thuds" were in a conflict complicated enough to qualify for science-fiction. Elaborate battle plans, flak-suppression missions, anti-missile flights and aerial refuelling developed, against very tough opposition from fighters, flak and surface-air missiles, into the most intricate air fighting in the world.

Bombing policy was controlled from political bases in Washington on an on-off basis dependent on the winds of political change, which hampered the effective use of airpower in its proper sphere.

The escalation of effort, the use of the helicopter as a battle mount (in an attempt to substitute air mobility for sound military tactics) the employment of aircraft at low-level in intense flak and the use of small spotters for forward air control of strikes at low level, cost the USAF dearly. Helicopter losses alone were reckoned in thousands.

In one respect, Vietnam was a triumph for air power. Casualty evacuation by air brought down battle deaths to an all-time low and aerial supply was brought to a high pitch. In this field, as in reconnaissance, peaceful benefits have resulted that somewhat compensate for the expense of military employment.

Aided by infra-red photography, electromagnetic sensing equipment and by great technical advances in the design of cameras and stereo-plotting instruments, aerial exploration and survey has added enormously to our knowledge of our environment. Among the benefits have been accurate mapping of inaccessible regions, determination of frontiers, geological survey, archaeological research, conservation of resources, and – in a highly specialised survey – the plotting of high-altitude weather as part of the Concorde programme.

Most of the pioneer work in this field has been done by Britain. Fairey and Hunting both control survey companies whose experience goes back to the mid-1920s. This is one field in which military technology has aided conservation and the acquisition of knowledge.

The Choppers

The **Sikorsky VS-300** flew first in September, 1939. Seen here in its intermediate design form in 1940 with the first tail rotor installation, it has a recognisable affinity with the **Bell 212** (*top*) of Hong Kong Air, shown in a typical situation over Hong Kong some 30 years later.

The development of rotating wing design, either gyroplane or helicopter (the gyroplane, unlike the helicopter, has separate sources of power for forward thrust and vertical lift), followed the same broad lines as that of fixed-wing aircraft, in that most of the basic principles had been discovered more than a century before the advent of a practical power plant turned theory into reality. The subsequent development of rotorcraft was slowed by the complexities of design that became evident in the production of a successful power transmission, and by the fact that adequate fixed-wing aircraft were available and were cheaper and simpler to operate.

The first successful gyroplane was Juan de la Cierva's **C.4 Autogyro** of 1923, in which this brilliant pioneer of rotating wing flight introduced the hinge system in the rotor head that

gives vertically and horizontally controlled flexibility to the rotor blades, necessary to achieve lift. There had been gyroplanes and helicopters that worked before this date, starting with the Bréguet-Richet and Cornu machines of 1907, but they were experimental.

It was Bréguet, the great French pioneer, who built the first practical helicopter with Dorand, in 1935. On this, speeds of 61mph and endurances of one hour were achieved. The significance of this aircraft has been rather obscured by the more spectacular German successes that followed with the **Focke-Wulf Fw 61**. In 1940–41, Igor Sikorsky designed and flew the **VS-300**, in America and this is generally regarded as the machine that was the basis of production helicopters. Sikorsky in this sense fathered the helicopter industry.

Because the helicopter not only derived lift from rotating the rotor blades, but generated thrust forward, sideways or backwards by tilting the rotor disc, it could achieve vertical take-off and landing and great flexibility of operation. It needed, however, greater power than comparable fixed-wing aircraft and was complicated to fly and to maintain. This made it very expensive to operate, so that initially its benefits were confined to military and governmental work, in fields such as rescue and operation in terrain where conventional aircraft could not go.

In the 1950s, however, the gas turbine began to be applied to the helicopter. This cheaper and simpler power plant caused a revolution in helicopter technology and meant the widening of its application as costs came down and reliability went up. In consequence, vertical take-off and landing (VTOL) – the helicopter's

greatest asset – has become a selling point, as well as its ability to hover and therefore to enable inspection of sites or delicate manœuvring to be carried out.

Helicopters are now in widespread use for survey, supply and construction, charter and airline work, rescue and inspection and are in increasing demand for executive use where flexibility and mobility are required away from conventional airfields.

A second breakthrough is about to take place, thanks to modern technology and metallurgy: the complex and limited rotor system of links and hinges, which effectively set a limit of about 200mph on top speeds, is being replaced by a rigid or hingeless rotor able to absorb far greater loads. With the addition of fixed lifting surfaces to partially unload the rotor in flight, the speed barrier has been broken.

The Working Classes

Typical of the "frontier" operations possible with modern light aircraft are these three widely differing scenes. The **Twin Otter**, a very successful de Havilland Canada design powered by two 650-hp Pratt and Witney PT6A turboprops, is seen operating from the 400 yard strip below the volcano on Saba Island in the Dutch Antilles. Apart from a monthly schooner, this STOL aircraft service is the island's only link with the rest of the Caribbean.

The **Air Parts Fletcher 1284** shown "dusting" in New Zealand is a new version of the American **Fletcher FU-24**, with an Air Research TPE 331 turboprop. New Zealand was a pioneer in top dressing with super phosphate and crop dusting with insecticides, the greater part of its rugged agricultural land being covered in this way.

The **Cessna 180** single-engined light four-seater shown is one of the Kenya Police Wing aircraft. Air Patrol for surveillance, rescue and police work has proved ideal in such relatively under-developed areas.

The aeroplane has much to answer for through its use as a military weapon, but it is also true that there are vast areas of the world that have been literally opened up by air transport. Pioneer or primitive settlements have often owed survival for one or all of their members to the swift transportation that the aircraft offers, turning weeks of travel into hours. Together with the radio, the aeroplane has been the main means of sustaining man in much of the Australian outback, the wilds of New Guinea and the desert places of the world.

Of all the operators that sprang up in Australia, none had a more exciting career than the two pioneers of flying in New Guinea. Following the gold rush, in the spring of 1927, Guinea Airways and Bulolo Goldfields Aeroplane Service ran fabulously successful freight and passenger runs to the goldfields. The greatest triumph was the flying-in to Bulolo Valley goldfield, by Guinea Airways, of a complete gold dredge, 2500 tons of it, piece by piece, in a three-engined **Junkers G 31**.

Typical of Australian outback services are the famous Flying Doctors. Started in 1928 with a **DH 50** from Qantas, the service became nation-wide in 1933, after being kept in being by the Presbyterian Inland Mission when government subsidies were withdrawn. The famous pedal-powered wireless, invented by Tregear, an Adelaide engineer, which kept outlying homesteads in touch with the service, was an indispensable aid. Flying hospital sisters were introduced in 1945, and since then several similar organisations have come into being.

The church were strongly behind the Flying Doctor service and so it was not surprising that Flying Missionary services should also flourish. Before the end of the Second World War, the Missionary Aviation Fellowship had been formed in the USA and Britain. Operating in Africa, British MAF has today an operational area covering most of north-eastern and East Africa, with a South African MAF also at work. In 1973, there were forty aircraft to transport the sick and carry food and medical supplies as well as other missionary activities – summed up by their title "Wings of Mercy".

Africa uses the aeroplane for sterner things, too. The Kenya police, for instance, run a series of Police Wings from scores of small landing strips that make the task of enforcing the country's laws very much easier.

Specialised aircraft such as the three-engined **de Havilland Drover** were developed for the Flying Doctor service, and recent advances in Short Take-Off and Landing (STOL) aircraft have had obvious applications. The **Britten-Norman Islander**, the **Short Skyvan** and the de Havilland-Canada STOL transports, the **Beaver, Otter** and **Twin Otter**, were all partly or entirely designed to meet the needs of air operations in undeveloped areas.

The Private Owners

In 1946 Britain, which had dominated the light aircraft market outside America, found herself with the remains of an impressed pre-war fleet and an industry that, with few exceptions, was too busy with large projects and cost-plus government contracts to bother with light aviation.

The French, their government concerned to retain an interest in the air among the population, and with the problem of recreating an aircraft industry that had been barely kept alive building German trainers and communications aircraft, took positive action. They continued to turn out the trainers and the liaison aircraft, which were handed over to flying clubs, and they instituted a subsidy scheme to encourage people to build and own aeroplanes and to help clubs train pilots.

By the 1950s, there was therefore a strong French industry and a very healthy home-builder sector. The American Big Three, Beech, Cessna and Piper, was beginning to get a foothold in Europe. In Britain, the major product was a pre-war American design, the **Auster**. **Cessnas** and **Pipers** began to appear in some numbers (many of the former assembled in France)

and the style of aircraft and of flying alike began to approximate to commercial practice.

The first major factor in this was the introduction, in the late 1950s, of the **Piper Comanche**, an all-metal, tricycle-undercarriage, low-wing cabin monoplane. Similar types appeared in a wide range of powers and sizes, and the light twin became popular. With increasing power, operation at altitude became possible and oxygen became a requirement. Weights increased with power so top speeds remained around 200mph.

In the 1970s, very few light aircraft in what is now called general aviation are without radio. Most carry at least one navigation aid, and many are equipped to nearly airline standard. With the availability of luxurious six-seater twins and larger aircraft, culminating in the small jets, executive and business flying has thrived.

With all this, the old original sporting values have not been entirely lost. International air rallies and races take place regularly and certain aspects such as aerobatics have not only become highly specialised and professional, but have achieved the status of World Championships.

Allied to the services illustrated on the preceding pages is the remarkable Swiss mountain rescue service pioneered by a great Swiss pilot, Hermann Geiger. Operating initially on his own with one of the ski-equipped **Piper Super Cubs** shown, he developed a technique for landing and taking off on snow slopes and glaciers which has led to the institution of a large organisation, founded on his individual efforts, from the little mountain airfield at Sion.

Aerobatics is really a subject by itself. It has existed almost as long as flying, the first loop being recorded in 1913. Many specialised aircraft have been developed, especially for the exact and demanding tasks of international competition. One of the major break-throughs came with this Czech **Zlin 226**, first of a continuing line of outstanding aerobatic aircraft. With this the Czechs swept the competition board in the 1950s and in 1973 the latest developed versions continued to provide the majority of mounts for national teams.

Gliding, too, is a subject of its own and – again in international competition – has produced some of the most refined and efficient airframes ever designed. The **Slingsby Skylark**, shown here with its faithful **Auster** tug, is one of a successful range of British sailplanes that became popular after the war. The **Auster** itself, tough, economical, austere and old-fashioned, nevertheless sold widely in many countries and was, during the late 1940s and 1950s the main British private aircraft.

The Airlifts

Isolated air drops took place in the First World War. The first major supply mission occurred when four **BE2Cs** of 30 Squadron and a **Voisin**, a **Henry Farman** and three **Short seaplanes** of the RNAS Flight dropped 19,000 pounds of food into Kut-el-Amara between 15th and 29th April, 1916. Intended to prolong the resistance of General Townshend's besieged forces, each aircraft carried between 100 and 200 pounds. On the first day they dropped 3350 pounds to the garrison.

Local drops of ammunition and water by **DH 4** and **DH 9** bombers to isolated troops were made on the western front in 1918, but the first genuine airlift operation designed to save life was the celebrated evacuation of Kabul during the rebellion of Habibullah Khan. When the British Legation became isolated,

Typifying the different uses of transport aircraft in war are the **Fairchild C-119 Packet** of Troop Carrier Command, Japan-based for employment in Korea and the more modern **Hercules** in Vietnam, delivering stores in an ultra-low level supply mission in a tactical rôle. Both types were converted into heavily armed "gun ships" for troop suppression missions — experiments that became established practice in Vietnam.

Sir Francis Humphrys, the Commissioner, asked that aircraft be flown in, as the Residency was under shell and rifle fire, to get the women and children away. Between 23rd December, 1928 and 25th February, 1929, 586 people were evacuated to Risalpur in India. The work was done principally by eight **Vickers Victorias** of 70 Squadron at Bagdhad, escorted through the Khyber Pass by 20 Squadron's **Wapitis**.

The end of the Second World War saw two notable airlifts. In the first, Operation Manna, 6684 tons of food was dropped to the Dutch by **Lancasters** and **Mosquitos** of Bomber Command between 29th April and 8th May, 1945. The situation had become acute because German demands had caused a strike of Dutch rail workers, and the German commander in the Netherlands, von Blaskewitz, agreed to a truce for the mercy flights.

Operation Exodus, the repatriation of prisoners of war, began on 4th May, 1945, and **Lancasters** flew 74,000 POWs home from Brussels and Juvincourt in the next 24 days.

On 24th June, 1948, the Russians, making their final move in a six-months' campaign to seal off Berlin, totally closed the land frontier, and the Anglo-American

air forces started to implement plans for supplying 2,100,000 west Berliners and their own occupying forces by air.

The airlift started on 26th June, with 80 tons sent in by USAF **Dakota**. (Just before the airlift, the USAF had merged its Air Transport Command with the Naval Air Transport Service to form Military Air Transport Service – MATS; its duties included weather, rescue, photo and airways and air communications services as well as a global network of routes.) By 15th July, 54 **C-54**s and 105 **C-47**s were lifting in up to 1500 tons daily. Berlin required 4500 tons though, and even with the British effort more was required. Eight squadrons of **C-54**s, 72 aircraft, were brought in by MATS and by the end of July the USAF was flying in 2000 tons a day. At the peak of their effort, the Americans had on average 225 **C-54**s (two Navy squadrons having joined in) operational out of a force of 319, pluss five **C-82**s, a **C-74** (briefly) and even on one occasion a **Liberator**.

On Monday, 28th June, an RAF **Dakota** from Wunstorf flew into Gatow in the British sector at 0600 hours. Thirteen **Dakotas** flew in that day, carrying 44 tons of food. The plan, until 4th July, was to fly in 440 tons a day in the **Dakotas** of 46 and 38 Groups, hurriedly sent out from England. After that date, when 37 Group's four-engined **Yorks** joined in, it would rise to 840 tons. In fact, at the end of July, it reached 1600 tons, then dropped to the forecast tonnage, rising again to 1000–1200 tons early in

the new year. In addition, civilian aircraft were called in from 28th July, and flew in an average of 112 tons a day, rising to a November peak of 450 tons and thereafter settling to 250–350 tons.

On February 18th, the millionth ton was flown in by a Transport Command **York**. On 16th April, the three airfields in the British sector handled a record 1398 landings and 12,940 tons. This included the many American aircraft that used the fields, and was a special effort.

Beside the **Dakotas** and **Yorks**, RAF **Sunderlands** and the new **Hastings** were employed, as well as civil **Haltons** and **Lancastrians**, **Freighters** and **Tudors**. Odd flights by a **Wayfarer** and some **Vikings** also took place.

The airlift ended at noon on 11th May, 1949. A total of 194,990 flights were made (two thirds by the USAF) with an average time between movements of about three minutes. 1,582,685 short tons had been flown into Berlin.

During the Korean war, MATS perfected the art of airborne supply and created a helicopter rescue service of which one unit – 3rd Air Rescue Squadron – made 9680 recoveries of personnel in the combat area, 996 of them from behind the enemy lines. They established a trans-Pacific supply line, borrowing civil transports to reach a total of 250 **C-54**s.

After the war, the Americans built up a turboprop fleet of **Hercules** tactical transports and the lessons learned in Korea were developed in Vietnam.

The Great Freighters

Economically and ecologically, it was inevitable that only the Soviet Union and the United States of America should have developed the giant freight aircraft to the point at which it stood in the early 1970s. No other nations could either support or employ such very large units. The military requirement of airlifting ever larger numbers of troops or quantities of material was the familiar origin of these aircraft – but only the state of the design art and the power of available engines has made it possible to build aircraft that will fly not only such heavy, but such extremely bulky loads.

The **Lockheed C-5A Galaxy** (*left*) has a span of 222 feet and is powered by four 41,000-lb-thrust General Electric turbofans, giving it a speed of 570mph. Landing problems are taken care of by 28 main wheels, whose tyres can be deflated in flight to provide greater bearing surface for soft ground.

Most fantastic of all the big transports are the **Guppies**. This **Super Guppy**, designed by On Mark Engineering for Aero Space Lines, is unloading the S-IVB third stage of a Saturn V rocket. Converted from one of two **C-97J Stratocruisers** with 7000-eshp turboprop engines, this 1965 design has a 25-foot high cargo hold.

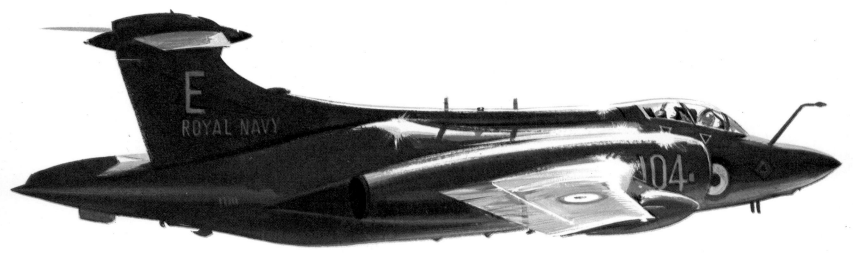

A series of typical operations undertaken by the British forces. *Top left* a **Vulcan** of one of Strike Command's Waddington Wing of three squadrons in No 1 Group swings away from a refuelling link with a **Victor T. Mk 2** of the Command tanker Wing (three squadrons) at Marham.

Below this, one of the Royal Navy's **Buccaneer** strike aircraft (with their Phantoms, the last of their fixed wing squadrons in current terms). Some 65 of these low-level twin-engined strike/attack aircraft, of very long range, have been handed over to the

Below again, a **Westland Lynx** is seen landing on HMS Blake. Developed as an 8–10-seater helicopter for Army, Navy and Royal Marines (and the French) it embodies lessons learned from Suez and Malaysian operations. The small illustration on the opposite page shows one of the RAF's maritime reconnaissance **Nimrods**, developed from the **Comet**. In the larger picture is a **VC-10** of No 10 Squadron, based at Brize Norton, engaged in night trooping operations. The squadron, the only one equipped with the **VC-10**, employs 14 of them to fulfil the RAF's requirements for a personnel carrier for Strike Command to the Far East, and runs trans-Atlantic schedules as well.

The New Royal Air Force

With the reshaping of RAF Commands and the phasing out of fixed-wing aircraft in the Royal Navy – as well as with the eventual disappearance of their carriers – the British forces in the world have had to display considerable adaptability.

After the post-war run-down in the RAF, rearmament began with the introduction of jets, and the number of fighter squadrons was greatly increased during the Korean crisis. The decision to arm the RAF with nuclear weapons and the entry into service of the V-bombers, **Valiant**, **Victor** and **Vulcan**, from 1955, gave Britain a nuclear deterrent and a prime role in NATO. American Thor intermediate range ballistic missiles thickened-up the V-bomber force from 1958 to 1963, but the planned acquisition of Skybolt air-launched ballistic missiles, to stretch the operational

service of the V-force, fell through when the Americans abandoned the missile. Polaris missiles were provided instead for Royal Navy submarines and, when these became operational in 1969, the V-bomber force transferred to a tactical role with NATO. In 1973, this meant the Waddington Wing of 1 Group, Strike Command, comprising three **Vulcan** squadrons. **Valiants** were scrapped in 1965 and the remaining **Victors** became Strike's tanker force at Marham.

With the loss of overseas bases and the decision by planners in the early 1960s to give priority to the mobility conferred by air transport, a Strategic Reserve was created in the UK to be lifted to trouble spots by the RAF. **Britannias**, **Comets** and **Argosies** of Transport Command had plenty of practice in taking troops to brush wars. No. 38 Group, reformed in 1960 as a tactical force working with the army, was able to perfect its techniques in Kuwait in 1961, in Brunei in 1962, in Borneo during the Indonesian confrontation from 1962 to 1966, in South Arabia and at Aden. In the mid 1960s a major re-equipment began for all Commands. The **Buccaneer** replaced the **Canberra**, the Mach-2 **Phantom** and **Lightning** (two of the world's finest fighting aircraft) replaced the **Hunter**, and **Hercules** (tactical) and **VC10** and **Belfast** (strategic) transports replaced the ageing **Argosies**. **Nimrod**, the first pure jet long-range maritime aircraft, took over from the **Shackleton**. On the order books were the revolutionary **Harrier** and the Anglo-French **Jaguar**. New and advanced helicopters were introduced.

With all this, the structure of the RAF was completely reshaped. Bomber and Fighter Commands merged into Strike Command in April, 1968, absorbing Signals and Coastal Commands during 1969. Air Support Command (Transport's new name since August, 1967) merged with Strike in September, 1972, and the RAF's operational force became one, multi-purpose unit.

The decision to wind up the carrier force of the Royal Navy when the through-deck cruisers were scheduled to replace Ark Royal in 1978 was a bitter blow to Naval Air. Hermes was converting to a commando rôle in mid-1973, to replace Albion (up for disposal) and with the end of Ark the end of fixed-wing naval aircraft was also to be seen. The process had already begun in the early 1970s with the transfer of **Phantoms** and **Buccaneers** to Strike Command. The helicopters remained, **Sea King, Wessex, Wasp** and **Lynx**, on cruisers, destroyers and frigates, but considering the magnificent record of carrier-borne support in all British involvements since the war, the abolition of that force was a hard, and to many in the Royal Navy, an incomprehensible blow.

The Commuters

General aviation and third level operations cover a very wide field, with aircraft ranging from the single engined four seater **Cessna** taxi, seen from the tower of an Australian airfield, to the Ansett Airways **Fokker Friendship Series 200** with 48 seats, at the other end of the scale. The curious, but effective, **Britten-Norman Trislander** was developed (*upper right*) from the British company's **Islander**, of which over 400 had been sold, mostly for export, by May, 1973. It entered service with Aurigny Airlines on Channel Island routes in 1972.

The **Hawker Siddeley HS 125**, of which the **Series 600** increased performance and capacity version is shown (*below*) is a British executive jet that has sold extremely well in the USA.

The term "general aviation", adopted in the United States some years ago, covers every non-scheduled type of civil operation. Besides private, executive and business flying, it embraces crop dusting, charter and other commercial operations. In Britain, the same phrase excludes any commercial operation, whether scheduled or non-scheduled. Neither definition includes third-level or feeder services when, as is usually the case, they operate to fixed timetables, but the same types of aircraft may well serve general aviation as well as scheduled services.

Third-level or commuter services had not, by 1973, become common outside the USA, where they carried 4·9 million passengers, using 675 multi-engined aircraft, in 1971. The original specification for these services, set out by the Civil Aeronautics Board (CAB) in 1952, restricted them to aircraft weighing less than 12,500 pounds (above that weight, more severe operating conditions obtain) to prevent possible competition with the regular airlines.

At the beginning of 1972, commuter airlines began to press for amendment of these regulations as traffic expanded, and Alleghany Airlines was granted an exemption to enable it to use 26-seater **Aérospatiale 262**s instead of its 15-seaters. In July, Part 298 CAB amendment established a new top operating limit of 30 passengers or 7500-pound payload.

As the third-level lines operate chiefly in very crowded airspace, draining off the concentrations of passengers generated by the big jets, CAB obviously felt it better to increase aircraft capacity rather than aircraft numbers. Commuter services are growing fast and should begin to flourish in Europe by the later 1970s. They stimulate the development of medium-size twin-engined aircraft of interesting and useful design. In 1973, the majority were **Beechcraft**, with 283 aircraft, but European work in this field is well advanced and such aircraft as the **Aérospatiale (Nord) 262** and the Russian **Yak-40** are causing interest in the USA.

The Air Transport Game

The **Hawker Siddeley Trident 3** of BEA (*above*) is a high-capacity short-haul development of the original **Trident 1E**. Its most significant feature is the fitting of the very advanced British Autoland system. This fully-automatic blind landing system, fitted in its "Category 3B condition" form enables the **Trident** to be landed fully on instruments under very adverse weather conditions, down to a decision height (to land or not to land) of 12 feet, with a Runway Visual Range (RVR) as low as 750 feet.

Before 1939, the operation of an international airline was a comparatively simple affair. Traffic demands were light, routes were for the most part aligned with national needs and did not greatly clash with the interests of other airlines. On a purely national level, in Britain and America, where a number of smaller, free-enterprise operators were fighting for survival, it was another matter.

The introduction of large numbers of people to air transport during the war and the arrival of the aircraft as a commonplace in most people's lives, led inevitably to a great expansion in air travel when the airlines were re-established.

The ability of the aeroplane to provide easy international travel led to political and technical problems of an entirely new nature – although people were beginning to accept the fact that national boundaries and differencies were not the final things they had once seemed to be.

The abortive Dominion Conference of 1943, called by Lord Beaverbrook to settle a future international policy, did establish some basic rules regarding the right to operate internationally and generate traffic in other people's countries. Adopted as the Five Freedoms, with later additions, they have become the accepted regulations for establishing international routes.

The 1944 Chicago Conference to discuss airline problems led to the formation of the International Civil Aviation Organisation (ICAO), which is responsible for formulating policies and recommending practices for the safe conduct of commercial flying. Wide differences in national outlooks and methods point the need for ICAO.

Another body, formed a year later, was the International Air Transport Association (IATA), a voluntary organisation to which almost all international airlines belong, dedicated to the prevention of unfair – and possibly unethical – methods of competition in fare-fixing and schedule operation. The factors affecting the running of a modern airline are basically that it must carry increasing numbers of passengers to stay solvent; that it must attract passengers by safety, speed and regularity of operation; and that it must, in consequence, try to be a step ahead of competitors with its equipment and its methods.

Under these conditions, and with the limitations of aircraft design, it is only practical to choose either to carry much larger numbers in a single aircraft, with the Jumbos and wide-bodied jets, or to carry them very much faster, with supersonic airliners. The great majority of airlines, taking only one step forward at a time, have chosen the high-density, very large airliner. Supersonic air travel requirers an act of faith that few, in 1973, seemed willing to make.

The larger the aircraft, the fewer are required, and therefore, in order to maintain schedules without a number of idle units, the greater the engineering and maintenance effort required to achieve full utilisation.

With aircraft carrying 500 or more passengers over well-defined routes, in and out of crowded focal areas, safety has become a critical feature of airline operation. While the control of air traffic is not the business of airlines, they have introduced complicated and advanced systems of blind flying and elaborate navigational aids, in order to operate under all weather conditions. An example of the most advanced aid to all-weather capability has been the pioneer introduction of Autoland on the **Tridents** of British European Airways.

As airliners and air operations became more complicated, the duties of pilots became increasingly onerous. Through the recommendations of ICAO, airline crews have been given rigid limitations of duty hours, flying times and rest periods, and the question of pilot fatigue and health is constantly recurring. The most elaborate training structure has grown up within each airline to provide fresh crews and to exercise constant proficiency checks on personnel.

With the prime business of an airline (apart from profitable survival) being the generation of traffic, passenger handling has grown to the status of a separate industry, like engineering and crew training. Often centralised round a computer, the booking and processing of the millions of airline passengers each year over complex routes, with interchanges, is a constant headache of administration.

Airline operations have separated into a number of clear and self-supporting channels. To the international and national airlines have recently been added a swiftly-growing charter and inclusive-tour business and third-level or feeder lines, occupied principally with the dispersal of traffic to various destinations from major arrival centres. These newcomers are usually in the hands of separate operators. Also run as a separate operation, though sometimes combined with passenger traffic, is an expanding freight business.

These channels, through the requirements of operators, have tended, in the 1960s and 1970s to dictate the design of aircraft, a notable example being the specialised requirements formulated by American Airlines for short-range, high-density work in the eastern United States that gave rise to the **Tri-star** and **DC-10**.

The cockpit illustration, of a **Boeing 707**, gives an idea of the complexity of modern airliner "offices". The Captain traditionally occupies the left-hand seat, the First Officer the right-hand one, with the Flight Engineer at his own panel of engine instruments behind. Instrument layout is standardised, flight instruments duplicated before each pilot, engine controls and radio between them, with a bewildering mass of switches and controls for ancillary equipment in the roof.

The Guiding Hand

This panorama of Schipol Airport, Amsterdam, might be repeated at any major air terminal in the world, so standardised and impersonal has the whole scene become. Visible are a **DC-10** of KLM, a **747** of Lufthansa, a **DC-8** of SAS, a **DC-9** of Alitalia and an **Airbus A-300B** of Iberia.

The question of controlling flying did not enter men's minds until the start of commercial flying in 1919. Before that time, there had been control only in the sense of prohibition, the governments of most countries having established prohibited zones over defence installations. As all flying had been in the private sector, always the most sensitive to control from outside, and the number of aircraft flying had been very small, the question had not been raised.

With the start of commercial airlines and the introduction of air routes between major cities, it was soon obvious that steps would have to be taken to ensure safety. Very simple rules were sufficient in those early days of slow aircraft, infrequent services and total lack of navigational aids. Even radio was only gradually introduced into airline operation. As flying became more intense and aircraft speeds greater, and as the numbers of passengers increased the complexity of control rose to conform with the acceleration of activity.

While it is under control, every aircraft has to be separated by defined distances, vertically, horizontally and temporally, from other traffic. It is on this principle that the safety of operations is based.

Because there is usually only one major airport at any city, and all aircraft going between that and any other airport naturally want to use the shortest route, traffic became channelled and concentrated at the departure and arrival points. This created a collision hazard that would have been almost unknown in random

flight over the rest of the sky, and was the reason for nearly all the control regulations that have been introduced. Up to a point, concentration is a benefit to air traffic controllers, whose main requirement is to know precisely and with the least delay exactly where all the aircraft in their area are and where they are going. The present system of Air Traffic Control (ATC) has grown out of these problems.

This evolution has only neared its completion since the Second World War. International bodies such as ICAO have established certain principles on which a fully international system has been built up. It was obviously not easy to reach universal agreement on such vital questions as the official language of ATC (which is English). Nor was it, at first, easy

to get acceptance of the essential requirement for safe operation, that ATC directions are mandatory.

The present system of control is operated mainly from the major airports, where concentration of traffic is the greatest, and facilities for ground installations are easiest to provide. The method of operating control is basically the same, whatever the size of the airport.

Every airfield, from minor local aerodromes to the commercial airports (except the small, private airstrip), has an "aerodrome zone": a drum of air around it, within which the movement of aircraft entering or leaving is protected and manipulated by an Air Traffic Control Officer. At major airports, this operation is divided into three sections, working from different control

rooms with radio communication and radar to keep traffic moving in accordance with the rules.

On the ground, an aircraft is directed by Ground Control, switching to a different set of frequencies in the Control Tower for take-off or landing and coming under the direction of Approach Control on a third set of frequencies for the portion of the flight between the airport and the Airways. Airways are ten-mile-wide corridors, some 20,000 feet in depth, along which airliners are routed, each on its own level, separated horizontally by time intervals. Once established on an Airway, control is effected by an ATC unit away from the aerodrome, over areas of the sky split up into Flight Information Regions.

The Boeings of Seattle

After the war, Boeing swung back into the lead in airliner production, with the introduction of jet power.

The firm had considerable expertise in utilising military designs for civil purposes. The **Type 314** used the **XB-15** wing and engines, the **Stratoliner** those of the **B-17**, the **Stratocruiser** those of the **B-29**. It was not surprising, therefore, that the radical **B-47** jet bomber of 1947 (which owed quite a lot to German research and development) should in 1954 give birth to a civil airliner. Like the **Stratocruiser**, much of the development and production cost was absorbed by prior military orders.

The production Boeing **707** appeared in many varieties, with different characteristics of range, power and passenger capacity.

A short-range, lighter version was developed as the **Model 720**, almost identical in appearance, which led to a specialised new aircraft for the lucrative short and medium-range market, the three-engined **727**, carrying up to 119 tourist class passengers. It later appeared in a stretched version with 34 per cent increased capacity.

Still in the short-range sector, at about the same time in 1965 that the 727 became available, production of the **737** began, springing from the three-engined design, though outwardly very different, with two flush-mounted under-wing engines of 14,000-pound thrust and 99 passengers, later increased to 103–115 in the **-200** series. Over 320 had been ordered by April, 1972. Alert to the growing requirements for a high-capacity, long-range commercial transport, Boeing evolved the **Model 747**, with double the **707**'s seating at 382 passengers, 43,000 to 47,000-pound thrust turbofans and a range of 6000–7000 miles.

Four members of the prodigious
Boeing family of jet airliners. Below
the great **747** are the short/medium-
haul three-engined **727**, the twin-
engined short-range **737** and the **707**,
which was the highly successful
progenitor of the range.

The Quiet Americans

The arrival of the new quiet, wide-bodied jets like the **Lockheed TriStar**, seen here in Court Line's colourful livery, has made possible great increases in charter and inclusive-tour traffic. Luton-based Court were, in conjunction with Clarkson's Tours, the first inclusive-tour operators to put the **TriStar** to work, early in 1973.

Overleaf, **Concorde** in the majestic setting of London's City and dockland.

Following the introduction of the Jumbo jet on long-range operations, it was predictable that the same way of absorbing increasing passenger loads would apply to short-haul routes as well. Lockheed-California started studies for an aircraft to sell in this sector in 1966, their design being considerably influenced by requirements published for the Chicago–Los Angeles route by American Airlines.

Part of the requirement was for take-off from existing, comparatively short runways at full load, which would require a good deal of power, and Lockheed settled for three of the Rolls Royce RB-211 high bypass-ratio, three-shaft turbofan engines in the **L-1011 TriStar**. Each engine develops 42,000-pound thrust, which gives the aircraft a maximum speed at top weight of Mach 0·9 at 30,000 feet.

The **TriStar**, like the **Douglas DC-10**, designed to fairly similar requirements, has introduced a new type of airliner, the wide-bodied jet, over a very broad spectrum of routes. The **DC-10** is intended for route lengths of from 300 to 6000 miles, requiring great flexibility of operation. The **TriStar** seats up to 400 economy-class passengers in 6, 8, 9 or 10 abreast seating and can operate up to 42,000 feet, significantly higher than previous airliners.

It had obvious applications in the expanding charter/inclusive-tour industry and Court Line in Britain ordered five in 1971 to operate for Clarkson's Tours. They were the first tour operators to buy the aircraft, followed by LTU in Germany. Total orders in mid-1973 were for 199 aircraft, from such airlines as BEA, TWA, Air Canada and All Nippon. Whatever the ultimate destiny of **Concorde**, it is sure of its niche in history, for it is the most controversial aircraft in the world.

The agreement for the production of two prototype, two static test and two pre-production aircraft of this SST was signed on 29th November, 1962. Agreements between British Aircraft Corporation (BAC) and the Société Nationale Industrielle Aérospatiale (SNIAS) to build the airframes and between Rolls-Royce, Bristol

Engine Division and the Société Nationale d'Etude et de Construction de Moteurs d'Aviation (SNECMA) to build the engines, followed.

Concorde was being enthusiastically supported by the British and French governments and the United States President was urging a reluctant nation to compete, fearing a setback to national pride if there was no American SST. The Soviet Union was building prototypes of their own SST, the Tupolev Tu-144, faster than Concorde but with fewer passengers. It flew, in fact, just over two months before 001.

Then costs began rocketing from the first, blind estimate of £150 million (shared equally by France and Britain.) The British share alone quickly reached that figure, with an estimated total revised to £500 million. In an effort to halt this trend, the French director was replaced. In Britain, a newly-elected Labour government immediately tried to cancel the programme altogether, but found that the open-ended contract contained no break clause, neither side could

opt out.

In spite of Presidential backing, the American SST programme faded away. Unable to finance a viable project themselves and unwilling to accept "nationalisation" in the form of government participation, the US industry and government opted out.

Concorde, for good or ill, continued, becoming more and more the symbol of united European hopes of breaking the US stranglehold on commercial aviation. The first of the pre-production aircraft, 01, flew at Filton, BAC's assembly plant, on 17th December, 1971 and the airline option book stood at 74.

The first British prototype (002, built at Filton) had flown on 9th April, 1969, and the second pre-production aircraft from Toulouse, Concorde 02, on 10th January, 1973. Up to the 10th July, 1973, the various aircraft had accumulated 1853 hours of flight time, 525 of them supersonic.

In the meantime, two things had happened. The Soviet Tu-144 being demonstrated at the Salon

de l'Aéronautique at le Bourget crashed on Sunday, 3rd June, 1973 during the final flying display, under circumstances that led to wide speculation on the soundness of the design (which had undergone major modification) and this inevitably affected the public view of all SSTs. Almost simultaneously, one by one and starting with the United States, the airlines interested in Concorde cancelled their options, until Air France and BOAC were left alone.

The New Ways of War

15,000lb of stores and an M61-A1 Vulcan 20mm cannon with 1000 rounds make the **Vought A-7E Corsair II** a powerful weapon. Designed for the US Navy as a carrier-based close support replacement for the **Skyhawk**, the first of a planned series of 500 aircraft entered service in 1969.

The result of the application of air power in the Korean and Vietnam wars was to concentrate attention in military planning on close support and battlefield strike operations. While long-range nuclear deterrent forces continued in being, there appeared to be, in early 1973, practical moves at last towards acceptance of the futility of large-scale nuclear war.

The Strategic Arms Limitations Talks (SALT) were begun by the USA and USSR in the first months of 1970 and the Treaty implementing them was signed in Moscow on 26th May, 1972. Made possible by the existence of reconnaissance satellites on both sides which can monitor missile escalation, it would seem to underline the presumption, in the 1970s and probably beyond, that future conflicts would continue to be of the "brush fire" variety.

The successful development of modern support/strike aircraft has been largely due to the enormous increases in power available, which, combined with the philosophy of carrying stores externally on hard points, has held down the weight of the 1970s designs to around 32,000 pounds (for the **Jaguar**), compared with the 58,000 pounds of the very successful **Phantom**. The simplicity of the external stowage load system (which for a limited variety of stores was common German practice in the Second World War) has led to extreme flexibility of purpose.

Although this ability to carry bombs, rockets, missiles, gun or reconnaissance packs and other items has led to the true multi-rôle combat aircraft (MRCA), the increasing sophistication of the weapons has led to some divergence of opinion as to whether development potential ought to be sought in them rather than in the aircraft itself. Parallel with these weapons and platforms there has been a development, essential to the proper use of such fast, powerful weapon systems, of a variety of "black boxes". The various navigational and attack systems, gyro-stabilised and Doppler-radar assisted, feed into central computer systems that maintain the aircraft in its proper flight envelope en route to a target

selected and tracked by the system. The same system can aim, prepare and launch the appropriate weapons, presenting navigational or attack data to the pilot on a "head-up" display projected on to the windscreen.

The MRCA concept has meant that the distinctions between aircraft designed for different tasks has virtually disappeared – a process that began with the **Phantom**, originally developed as a long-range, all-weather attack fighter for the US Navy. Different versions in service with the US Navy, Royal Navy, RAF, Japanese Defence Agency, US Marines, USAF and Federal German Luftwaffe include two-seat air superiority, long-range and close support/attack fighters, shipboard fighter, and multisensor reconnaissance. The aircraft is also in service with the Imperial Iranian Air Force, Republic of Korea Air Force and Israeli Air Force. Capable of more than Mach 2 in level flight, the **Phantom** has seen service in Vietnam, and has more recently been tried out in dummy runs against Egyptian **Foxbats** over

the Mediterranean.

Foxbat is the NATO codename for the Soviet **Mikoyan MiG-25** all-weather fighter, developed from the record-breaking **E-266** of 1965. In 1967, it set up a speed record of 1852mph and the service version is credited with Mach 3 capability. Soviet-manned **MiG-25s** have been in Egypt since 1971, and it is not surprising that the previous-generation **Phantoms** failed to intercept any of their reconnaissance flights.

Very little is known in detail of **Foxbat**, but it seems likely that it may prove to be a superior aircraft to the **F-14** and **F-15**, the US designs that are intended to replace existing fighters in the USAF and US Navy inventories.

The **McDonnell Douglas F-15** is an air superiority fighter for the USAF, which can also be used in the attack rôle. Maximum speed is Mach 2 plus. Like **Foxbat**, it is intended to stop enemy strike aircraft. The **Grumman F-14 Tomcat** is a new carrier-based fighter for the US Navy, powered by two 20,000-pound thrust turbofans and capable of more

than Mach 2. Replacing the **Phantom** in the fleet in 1973, it has defence and strike responsibilities beside its main purpose of fighter escort for carrier strike forces. Production of the fifth and last lot of the current order of 134 aircraft was delayed by financial problems, but a solution to the differences over contract prices was resolved in March 1973.

The US Navy continued to plan an expanding carrier force, armed with powerful attack/strike aircraft such as the 700-mph **LTV Corsair 2** (also a veteran of Vietnam), with 15,000 pounds of stores. The political decision that Britain could not afford the planned CVA-01 carrier and that existing carriers were unsuitable for future tasks, brought the end of the Royal Navy's seaborne attack force in sight. British naval air activity after the 1970s will be restricted, it seems, to helicopter close cover to the fleet. Attack and defence against enemy strikes will be undertaken by land-based RAF squadrons.

The **English Electric Lightning** (*top*), later the **BAC Lightning**, was the RAF's first Mach-2 aircraft and has been their main All-Weather Fighter since early in the 1960s. Like the **Phantom** below it, it is a twin-engined aircraft. The **Phantom**, successor to the **Lightning**, was already in service with the USAF, USN and USMC — an unique distinction for a combat aircraft — and has become noted as one of the best fighting aircraft yet. Seen here in USAF colours, it carries the 20mm Vulcan gun in an under-fuselage pod and can lift 11 1000-lb bombs or their equivalent. The **Saab Viggen**, (*bottom*) was developed by Sweden's excellent aircraft industry to meet its peculiar needs for a sophisticated supersonic fighter capable of operating off small airfields. Single-engined, it has one of the most highly-developed, computerised navigation, attack and pilotage electronic systems in the world.

The Flexible Fighters

Representative of a spread of fighter/attack design covering the past twenty years, and a probable further ten years into the future, are the **Hawker-Siddeley Harrier GR Mk 1**, the BAC-**Bréguet Jaguar** and the **McDonnell Douglas A-4 Skyhawk**. Each represents a different breakthrough in military aircraft design or production.

The **Harrier** gave the RAF the world's first vertical/short take-off and landing (V/STOL) fixed-wing aircraft. With a top forward speed of Mach 0·95 and the ability to move quickly sideways and backwards and to hover, carrying 5000 pounds of stores and with

comprehensive electronic navigation and attack systems, it combines the ability of the helicopter to operate from small natural clearings near a battle area with the very quick close support reaction of a near-supersonic fighter. An integral auxiliary power unit gives it complete support independence. The RAF had one squadron and the Harrier Operational Conversion Unit at Wittering, and three squadrons in Germany in mid-1973, with another forming.

Jaguar was the first successful international military aircraft to be ordered in quantity. Designed by SEPECAT, a BAC-Breguet

aviation company and Rolls-
Royce Turboméca, the joint
engine company that produced
Jaguar's two 7000-pound thrust
Adour turbofans, it is supersonic,
carries two 30mm Aden guns and
10,000 pounds of stores. 400 have
been ordered, 200 for the French
Armée de l'Air and Aéronavale,
200 for the RAF. The first aircraft
of the RAF order flew in late 1972.
The latter was for 165 single-
seaters, to re-equip nine **Phantom**
squadrons, and 35 two-seat
trainers. The first production
aircraft were going through the
factory in March, 1973.

The diminutive **Skyhawk** was
planned as a jet replacement for
the **Skyraider** and was to be as
light and simple an attack
aircraft as the **Skyraider** was
heavy and complex. It first flew
in 1954 and 2000 were delivered
to the US Navy in the next
thirteen years. In 1973, it was in
service with eight air forces and
navies, including Israel, and had
been the very successful principal
ground attack, carrier-borne Navy
aircraft during the Vietnam war.
It is capable of carrying nuclear
or conventional bombs, rockets,
missiles or a torpedo and has
been progessively updated with
Elliott head-up display, terrain
avoidance radar, Doppler/inertial
navigational system and electronic
counter-measures.

The New Geometry

The **North American X-15** (*left*) provided much data for NASA for the later **Lockheed YF-12A/SR-71** (*above*). The **Northrop HL-10 lifting body** (*below*) with other similar designs will investigate problems of controlled manned re-entry from space with the carefully shaped body contours generating the lift normally produced by conventional wings.

With tremendous strides being made in technology and in engine design in the early 1970s, there are indications that the end of Euclidean aircraft design is in sight. For the first time in the history of flight, designers have more power available than they know what to do with, and not only can they explore entirely new areas of design but they are virtually forced to seek radically new solutions in order to achieve competitive performance.

While the jet engine was the first great step forward, the development of the multi-spool, multi-shaft, bypass turbofan engine in various forms is producing prodigious amounts of thrust and – a very useful spin-off indeed – doing it extremely quietly.

The advent of the silent-running bypass engine and the increasing environmental lobbying about noise has given rise to the Quiet Take-off and Landing (QTOL) concept. By the end of 1972, design studies were being investigated by Aeritalia-Boeing, Europlane (a consortium of BAC, Messerschmitt, Saab and Casa) and a Hawker-Siddeley-Fokker-DFW-Dornier group.

Variations on the STOL theme include the French **Bréguet 941S** military transport, achieving STOL with a 650-foot take-off run at 48,000 pounds weight by the use of deflected slipstream over the extensively slotted and flapped wing. Variations in this theme include the **Bell X-22A** research aircraft with tilting ducted propellers, the **Canadair CX-84** with a wing/engine group pivoting through 100°, the shrouded-propeller **Nord 500** and the tilt-rotor research projects ordered by the National Aeronautics and Space Administration (NASA) and the US Army from Bell and Boeing.

Built almost entirely of titanium or titanium alloys to withstand the sustained Mach 3 cruise of which the aircraft is capable and with an airframe of very advanced geometry, the **YF-12A** is armed with eight guided missiles and powered by two 32,500-pound thrust engines. A reconnaissance version, which it is believed was intended to replace the **U-2** until satellite surveillance became possible, and heavier and longer-ranged than the **YF-12A**, is the **SR-71A**.

A height record greater than either of the two mentioned was set up on 17th July, 1962, by the **X-15A-3**, air-launched from a **B-52**. Flown by Major R. White, USAF, it reached 314 750 feet, or nearly 60 miles. The greatest height reached by **X-15** was 354 200 feet (67 miles). In the course of the 1959–69 research programme undertaken with the three built by North American, 199 flights were made and speeds of Mach 6·4 were reached.

NASA's vast programme of research into high speeds and extreme altitudes was directed towards the next generation of military aircraft, including the **B-70 Valkyrie** Mach 3 delta bomber and its successor, the **North American Rockwell B-1**, of which it is planned, following a successful first flight in 1974, to order 250 to replace SAC's **B-52**s. Cruising at high subsonic speeds (about Mach 0·85) and capable of reaching about Mach 2·2 at 50,000 feet, the 400,000-pound **B-1** will be powered by four 30,000-pound thrust turbofans.

The **B-1** design involves one of the most complex and tricky developments in contemporary aeronautical engineering: the swing wing. Swept to a shallow 15 degrees in the low-speed configuration, the wings retreat to an angle of 67 degrees 30 minutes for maximum speed.

The swing wing first came into prominence in the publicity surrounding Dr Barnes Wallis's **Swallow** airliner project, but the pioneer work was done by Messerschmitt during the war with Project 1101, which was subsequently sent to the USA and became the basis of the **Bell X-5**. The value of sweep-back to overcome compressibility effects at high Mach numbers led to the swept wing, and the need for a more conventional shape at low speeds has led to the variable-geometry or swing wing for very fast aircraft that still need to land slowly.

The **General Dynamics F-111** was the first variable-geometry aircraft to enter service. One of the most controversial aircraft of all time, it was plagued by changes of operational requirement and suffered a temporary eclipse following several losses through structural failures. **F-111s** served in Vietnam with the 428th Tactical Fighter Squadron, operating out of Thailand. A bomber development, the **FB-111A** entered operational service in 1970 as a replacement for the **B-52**, presumably pending the arrival of the **B1**.

The **F-111** first flew in 1964. In 1970, a second variable-geometry fighter, this time for the US Navy, was also flown. This was the **Grumman F-14 Tomcat**, with 20/75 degree sweep-back positions. In late 1972, two squadrons were activated to receive the **F-14** as a multi-mission carrier-borne fighter designed to combat **Foxbat**.

West Germany, Italy and Britain began design studies in 1969–70 for the **Panavia** MRCA, a variable-geometry, multi-rôle combat aircraft. The RAF is expected to acquire between 350 and 400 of this aircraft. In France, Avions Marcel Dassault – designers and builders of the very successful **Mystère/Mirage** series of fighter/bombers – flew the swing-wing **Mirage G** in 1967. This crashed in 1971 after some

The variable-sweep 'swing-wing" **Tomcat** (*above*) demonstrates maximum and zero degrees of sweep. The **Bréguet 941S** (*below*) has four Turboméca Turmo engines that provide slipstream over all the high-lift devices along the wing, while the Canadian **Canadair CX-84** tilt-wing provides vertical lift for take-off and landing.

400 hours of test flying, but it has led to the twin-engined v-g **Mystère G-8**. Three swing-wing prototype or research aircraft have flown in the Soviet Union, fighters from Mikoyan and Sukhoi and a bomber, in 1970, from Tupolev.

Most advanced of all projects in the early 1970s are the lifting-body research aircraft. These are wingless, rocket-powered designs, relying on lift generated at high speed by their specially shaped bodies.

In 1970–71 a series of test flights was made with the **Martin-Marietta X-24A**, launched from a **B-52** at about 45,000 feet and landing at speeds between 160 and 345mph. Another programme by Northrop/NASA resulted in flights about the same time with two research lifting-bodies, **M2-F3** and **HL-10**, while Martin developed the **SV-5B**, and in Germany ERNO produced the **Bumerang** in March, 1973.

These are preliminary studies for space shuttle programmes for which McDonnell Douglas/Martin Marietta, North American Rockwell/General Dynamics and Grumman/Boeing are competing.

The Outward Urge

On 4th October, 1957, the Soviet Union launched **Sputnik 1**, the first orbital satellite in history. Its weight astounded the United States scientists. 184 pounds was huge, compared to the 21-pound satellite being prepared in the USA.

In fact, Soviet launchers were much more powerful than their opponents' in the early years of spaceflight. Russian technology had not been competent to produce any but a massive and bulky warhead for the nuclear ICBM, and this had necessitated a powerful launcher adaptable to quite heavy satellite cargoes.

On 12th April, 1961, the first man to go into space was sent into orbit in the Soviet spaceship **Vostok** (East) **1**. Major Yuri Gagarin, in a flight of one orbit lasting 108 minutes, had earned a very significant place in history.

It is uncertain at what stage the Russians abandoned any plans for manned moon landings in the face of the accelerating lead of United States technology. Six **Vostok** one-man capsules were launched between 1961 and 1963. Fourteen months later, in the second of two **Voskhod** (Sunrise) spacecraft Lt.-Col. Leonov achieved the distinction of performing the first activity of man in space, outside a vehicle.

During this period, the United States completed the one-man Mercury programme, introducing the very successful Atlas D launcher (modified from their eventual ICBM) in the third launch. They then began the Gemini programme with two-man capsules, which ran to twelve launchings in 1964–66 and prepared the way for Apollo itself.

At the last Gemini launch and recovery in November, 1966, the USA had perfected a rendezvous-docking technique in space, developed an excellent control system for manoeuvring capsules and patently overtaken the Russians in 'know-how''. The two national programmes could now be seen to be on quite different lines: the USSR concentrated on development of an earth-orbiting space station, possibly to be built up in space, from which, craft could be sent to the moon and launched their **Soyuz** (Union) programme of eleven flights in 1967–71 to prepare for this.

Confronted with the same

problem of building rockets big enough to get men to the moon and back, NASA adopted the excellent method of setting up a *moon*-orbit station, from which the lunar capsule would be detached for its landing and which it could then rejoin for a combined return to earth. It was for this programme that the Gemini dockings and rendezvous were designed.

The Russians launched their orbital scientific station **Salyut** on 19th April, 1971, and achieved the first, brief docking with **Soyuz 10** three days later. A second attempt on 6th June gave the three man crew of **Soyuz 11** a record 24 days in space on board **Salyut**, but, tragically, a leaking hatch caused the death of all three on the return trip.

The Apollo programme also opened on tragedy, with three astronauts killed in a pre-launch fire in January, 1967, but eleven Apollo/Saturn rockets were fired between then and the return of the last Apollo astronauts from the Sea of Serenity.

The first manned rocket to reach the moon and land its crew was launched on 16th July, 1969. On the 21st, Neil Armstrong and Edwin Aldin made the first moon-walk in the Sea of Tranquillity. Early in 1973, the United States launched **Skylab**, a manned orbital station, in parallel to the still-circling **Salyut**. Using the third, S-IVB stage of a Saturn V booster as an orbital workshop, **Skylab** was crewed for a 28-day experiment by an Apollo command servicing module and airlock module lifted on a Saturn IB.

The splash-down of Captain Eugene Cernan, Dr Harrison Schmitt and Captain Ronald Evans in **Apollo 17** brought the first era of the Space Age to a close on 19th December, 1972 – sixty-nine years and two days after that momentous winter day at Kitty Hawk. Already plans exist for a joint US-USSR Apollo Soyuz Test Programme to conduct docking experiments with an Apollo module and Salyut between 10th and 18th June, 1975. US preparations for a space shuttle service are planned for 1979–80.

One would like to think that the gentle Wrights would have approved.

So to the end of our seventy years. The Wright biplane, weighing some 1000lb and 41 feet from tip to tip, has led to Apollo 17, a three-man spaceship, the culmination of a 16-year national effort that put a 364-foot-high spaceship up to the moon, at a lift-off weight of six million pounds.

Record Tables

The first in the set of tables that follows is a continuation of the last section, and sets out in some detail the record of man's ascent into space from the gravity-well of earth. The second is the story of "Fastest, farthest, highest" — the official records, confirmed by the Fédération Aéronautique Internationale for Speed, Distance and Altitude.

These records affirm the stage of development that had been reached by the aeroplane at a given time, for although in the majority of cases the aircraft were specially prepared and often specially designed, it was the stimulus of this mark of supremacy that helped to push research into the area of practical employment.

As flying developed, so did the type of record. Of the many thousands of records recognised over the years, only the "Absolute" or World records in the three most important categories have been listed. Prior to 1930, no distinction was made; after that date the most important were classified as Absolute World attempts, the remainder as World Class records in various categories.

Only a sample for detailed survey could be included from the numerous focal points of interest in aviation history — the great races, the pioneer flights, the individual stories of aircraft, of epics, of battles. One of the most important in all its implications, its international rivalry and its effect on the future history of flight, must be the Schneider Trophy race, and the tables end with this event.

MANNED SPACEFLIGHT
The Soviet Programmes
Programme 1 Vostok ("East")

12. 4.61	Vostok-1	Maj. Yuri Alexeyevich Gagarin First man in space; killed in air crash 27.3.68
6. 8.61	Vostok-2	Maj. Gherman Stepanovich Titov Manoeuvring tests with manual controls
11. 8.62	Vostok-3	Maj. Andriyan Grigoryevich Nikolayev Medico-biological tests
12. 8.62	Vostok-4	Lt. Col. Pavel Romanovich Popovich Launched to match Vostok-3 in orbit. No manoeuvring rockets and closest approach 4 miles. First group flight; first indication of Soviet space station interest
14. 6.63	Vostok-5 "Hawk"	Lt. Col. Valeri Fedorovich Bykovsky Bio-chemical and control tests; over 119 hours in space
16. 6.63	Vostok-6 "Seagull"	Hon. Jr. Lt. Valentina Vladimirovna Tereshkova Launched to match Vostok-5 orbit. Closest approach 3·1 miles. First woman in space; later married cosmonaut Nikolayev

Programme 2 Voskhod ("Sunrise")

12.10.64	Voskhod-1	Eng. Lt. Col. Vladimir Mikhailovich Komarov (commander), Dr. Boris Borisovich Yegorov, Konstantin Petrovich Feoktistov
18. 3.65	Voskhod-2	Col. Pavel Ivanovich Belyayev, Lt. Col. Alexei Arkhipovich Leonov Highest to date (308 miles). First space walk (Leonov) of 23min 41sec. Series abandoned and experience built into Soyuz. Belyayev died January, 1970

Programme 3 Soyuz ("Union")

23. 4.67	Soyuz-1	Col. Vladimir Mikhailovich Komarov Series devoted to perfecting space station techniques, testing new piloted spacecraft, medico-biological experiment. Komarov killed when parachute failed to deploy on re-entry
25.10.68	Soyuz-2	Unmanned
26.10.68	Soyuz-3	Maj. Gen. Georgi Timofeyevich Beregovoi Orbital rendezvous experiments with Soyuz-2. Manual controls; approached within several yards
14. 1.69	Soyuz-4	Maj. Gen. Vladimir Alexandrovich Shatalov
15. 1.69	Soyuz-5	Col. Boris Valentinovich Volynov, Alexei Stanislavovich Yeliseyev, Col. Yevgeni Vasilyevich Khrunov First docking experiments with Soyuz-4 under automatic control. Docked for 4hr 35min; Khrunov and Yeliseyev space-walked 1 hour
11.10.69	Soyuz-6	Col. Georgi Stepanovich Shonin, Valeri Nikolayevich Kubasov
	Soyuz-7	Col. Anatoli Vasilyevich Filipchenko, Col. Viktor Vasilyevich Gorbatko, Vladislav Nikolayevich Volkov
	Soyuz-8	Maj. Gen. Vladimir Alexandrovich Shatalov, Alexei Stanislavovich Yeliseyev Group flight with several changes of orbit. Shatalov mission commander, Shonin and Filipchenko other pilots. Automatic welding experiments in vacuum
1. 6.70	Soyuz-9	Maj. Andriyan Grigoryevich Nikolayev, Vitali Ivanovich Sevastyanov 424h 59min; record to date. Scientific, technical and bio-medical experiments
19. 4.71	Salyut	Orbital scientific station put in orbit
22. 4.71	Soyuz-10	Maj. Gen. Vladimir Alexandrovich Shatalov, Alexei Stanislavovich Yeliseyev, Nikolai Nikolayevich Rukavishnikov Rendezvous with Salyut, probably to refuel it
6. 7.71	Soyuz-11	Lt. Col. Georgi Timofeyevich Dobrovolski (commander), Vladislav Nikolayevich Volkov, Viktor Ivanovich Patasayev Docked with Salyut and entered spaceship. All three asphyxiated on return trip in Soyuz-11 when air lost through leaking hatch

The American Programmes
Programme 1 Mercury

9. 9.59	MA-1	Sub-orbital unmanned "boilerplate" Mercury firing with Atlas D launcher
29. 7.60		Second "boilerplate" launch, unmanned; booster blew up on pad
21.11.60	MR-1	First (abortive) Mercury/Redstone firing
31. 1.61	MR-2	Second Mercury/Redstone firing; sub-orbital carrying chimpanzee
21. 2.61	MA-2	Mercury/Atlas test firing
25. 4.61	MA-3	First orbital Mercury/Atlas firing; off course, destroyed
13. 9.61	MA-4	Successful one-orbit Mercury/Atlas test firing
29.11.61	MA-5	Successful two-orbit Mercury/Atlas flight, carrying chimpanzee
5. 5.61	MR-3	Cdr. Alan B. Shepard Jr., USN McDonnell Mercury/Redstone "Freedom 7" First non-orbital manned flight
21. 7.61	MR-4	Capt. Virgil I. Grissom, USAF McDonnell Mercury/Redstone "Liberty Bell 7" Sub-orbital
20. 2.62	MA-6	Lt. Col. John H. Glenn, USMC McDonnell Mercury/Atlas D "Friendship 7" First orbital manned US flight
24. 5.62	MA-7	Lt. Cdr. M. Scott Carpenter, USN McDonnell Mercury/Atlas D "Aurora 7"
3.10.62	MA-8	Cdr. Walter M. Schirra Jr., USN McDonnell Mercury/Atlas D 'Sigma 7''
15. 5.63	MA-9	Maj. L. Gordon Cooper Jr McDonnell Mercury/Atlas D "Faith 7" First American flight of over 24 hours; 22 orbits

Programme 2 Gemini

8. 4.64	GT-1	McDonnell Gemini/Titan 2 Unmanned sub-orbital test shot for system compatability; no separation
19. 1.65	GT-2	Unmanned separation test
23. 3.65	GT-3	"Molly Brown" Capt. Virgil I. Grissom, USAF (commander), Lt. Cdr. John W. Young, USN First spacecraft to manoeuvre into new orbit; Grissom becomes first "two-shot" spaceman
3. 6.65	GT-4	Maj. James A. McDivitt (commander), Maj. Edward H. White II, USAF First US Extra Vehicular Activity (EVA) or space walk. First link-up (unsuccessful) attempt, with second stage of Titan launcher
21. 8.65	GT-5	Lt. Cdr. Charles P. Conrad Jr., USN, Maj. L. Gordon Cooper Jr., USAF Beat Soviet 119hr record with 190h 56sec. Radar Evaluation Pod (REP) released
25.10.65	GT-6	Cdr. Walter M. Schirra Jr., USN (commander), Col. Thomas P. Stafford, USAF Launch abandoned when track lost of Lockheed Agena link-up target vehicle
4.12.65	GT-7	Lt. Col. Frank Borman, USAF (commander), Capt. James A. Lovell Jr., USN 14-day mission
15.12.65	GT-6	Cdr. Walter M. Schirra Jr., USN (commander), Thomas P. Stafford, USAF Second launch to rendezvous with GT-7; no contact
16. 3.66	GT-8	Neil A. Armstrong (commander), Maj. David R. Scott, USAF First successful docking with Agena target; problems terminated flight same day
17. 5.66	GT-9	Elliot M. See Jr. (commander), Capt. Charles A. Bassett, USN Postponed because Agena target lost
1. 6.66	GT-9	Elliot M. See Jr., Capt. Charles A. Bassett, USN Augmented Target Docking Adaptor (ATDA) launched, but fault in GT-9 and launch abandoned. Crew later killed in T-38 crash
3. 6.66	GT-9	Lt. Col. Thomas P. Stafford, USAF, Lt. Cdr. Eugene A. Cernan, USN Cernan 24h 9min EVA
18. 7.66	GT-10	Capt. John W. Young, USN (commander), Maj. Michael Collins, USAF Two dockings with Agena. First EVA contact with an orbiting object
12. 9.66	GT-11	Lt. Col. Richard F. Gordon, USAF, Cdr. Charles P. Conrad Jr (commander) Four docking/undocking sequences; experiments tying two ships together in orbit First automatically-controlled computer-steered splashdown. EVA on third day
11.11.66	GT-12	Maj. Edwin E. Aldrin, USAF, Cdr. James A. Lovell, USN (commander) At the end of the Mercury programme, US had 50 astronauts in training, had covered 17,616,000 miles in space to USSR's 7,471,000 miles

Programme 3 Apollo

26. 2.66	Apollo 1	Sub-orbital unmanned, launched by uprated Saturn I. North American Command Module (CM) and Grumman Lunar Exploration Module (LEM). Test of CM re-entry characteristics
	Apollo 2, 3	Similar tests
9.11.67	Apollo 4	"Boilerplate" LEM First successful Saturn V launch. Earth orbital
22. 1.68	Apollo 5	Saturn IB First test actual LEM
4. 4.68	Apollo 6	Saturn V Partially successful; first and second stages shut down prematurely, third failed to ignite
11.10.68	LEM 1/ Apollo 7 (SA-502)	Capt. Walter M. Schirra Jr., USN (commander), Maj. Donn F. Eisele (CM), Walter R. Cunningham (LM) First manned launch, Saturn IB, earth orbit, rendezvous tests with booster
21.12.68	LEM 2/ Apollo 8 (SA-503)	Col. Frank Borman, USAF (commander), Cdr. James A. Lovell Jr., USM (CM), Maj. William A. Anders, USAF (CM) This and all subsequent shots launched by Saturn V. First lunar orbital flight. Brought forward by NASA to anticipate Soviet unmanned Zond 5 and 6 moonshots
3. 3.69	LEM 3/ Apollo 9 (SA-504)	CM "Sundrop", LM "Spider" Col. James A. McDivitt, USAF (LM), Col. David R. Scott, USAF (CM), Russell L. Schweickart (LM) First test of LM in earth orbit; first complete test with Saturn booster/spacecraft
18. 5.69	LEM 4/ Apollo 10 (SA-505)	CM 'Charlie Brown", LM "Snoopy" Col. Thomas P. Stafford, USAF (commander), Cdr. John W. Young, USN (CM), Cdr. Eugene A. Cernan USN (LM) Last test of all systems before moon

16. 7.69 **LEM 5/** **Apollo 11** (SA 506)
CM "Columbia", LM "Eagle" Neil A. Armstrong (commander), Col. Edwin E. Aldrin Jr, USAF (LM), Lt. Col. Michael Collins, USAF (CM) Touchdown Sea of Tranquillity, first moon walk 21.7.69. 48lb of samples brought back

14.11.69 **LEM 6/** **Apollo 12** (SA-507)
CM "Yankee Clipper", LM "Intrepid" Cdr. Charles P. Conrad Jr, USN (commander), Cdr. Richard F. Gordon, USN (CM), Cdr. Alan L. Bean, USN (LM)
Landed Ocean of Storms, walked nearly 2 miles. First Apollo Lunar Surface Experiment Package (ALSEP) planted, 75lb samples brought back

11. 4.70 **LEM 7/** **Apollo 13** (SA-508)
Capt. James A. Lovell Jr, USN (commander), John L. Sweigert (CM), Fred W. Haise (LM)
Used LM "Aquarius" as lifeboat when service module oxygen tank exploded. Mission aborted

31. 1.71 **LEM 8/** **Apollo 14** (SA-509)
CM "Kittyhawk", LM "Antares" Capt. Alan B. Shepard Jr, USN (commander), Maj. Edgar J. Mitchell, USAF (LM), Cdr. Stuart A. Roosa, USN (CM)
Landed Fra Mauro crater; second ALSEP planted. Two moon walks of 4h 48min and 4h 41min respectively; 96lb samples brought back

26. 7.71 **LEM 9/** **Apollo 15** (SA-510)
CM 'Endeavour', LM "Falcon" Col. David R. Scott, USAF (commander), Col. James B. Irwin, USAF (LM), Lt. Col. Alfred M. Worden, USAF (CM)
Landed Appenines. Third ALSEP planted and first Boeing Lunar Roving Vehicle (LRV)) "Rover" landed, travelled 17 miles in 3 trips at Hadley Rille. 170lb samples brought back. On return Worden made first deep-space EVA 22,000 miles from earth
(This and next two shots were the "Expanded Capability" or Series J flights with LRVs and extended work programmes)

16. 4.72 **LEM 10/** **Apollo 16** (SA-511)
CM "Caspar", LM "Orion" Capt. John W. Young, USN (commander), Lt. Cdr. Thomas K. Mattingly, USN (CM), Lt. Col. Charles M. Duke, USAF (LM)
Fourth ALSEP and second LRV landed, ran 17 miles at average 10mph. Longest single EVA 7h 23min in total 20h 30min. 213lb of samples

7.12.72 **LEM 11/** **Apollo 17** (SA-512)
CM "America", LM "Challenger" Capt. Eugene A. Cernan, USN (commander), Dr. Harrison H. Schmitt (LM), Cdr. Ronald E. Evans, USN (CM)
Fifth ALSEP and third LRV landed and left on moon at end of mission

Programme 4 Skylab

14. 5.73 **Skylab 1** Launched unmanned. The Saturn V third stage (S-IVB) became Skylab Work Shop (SWS) in orbit. Apollo Command Servicing Module (CSM) and Airlock Module (AM) complete Skylab. Apollo Telescope Mount (ATM) carried

25. 5.73 **Skylab 2** Capt. Charles P. Conrad Jr, USN, Cdr. Joseph P. Kerwin, USN, Cdr. Paul L. Weitz, USN
Rendezvous Skylab 1, docked 26.5.73. Two main solar panels and meteorite shield on Skylab 1 had not deployed, but repairs carried out and full 28-day programme completed. Launched by Saturn 1B

28. 7.73 **Skylab 3** Capt. Alan L. Bean, USN (commander), Owen K. Garriott (science-pilot), Maj. Jack R. Lousma, USMC (pilot)
Second work team

WORLD RECORDS
FAI Records Class K
Manned Spacecraft

All measurements, being official FAI figures, are metric

Duration

		h.	min.	sec.
12. 6.61	Maj. Y. A. Gagarin Vostok-1 (USSR)		108	
6. 8.61	Maj. G. S. Titov Vostok-2 (USSR)	25	11	
11/ 15. 8.62	Maj. A. G. Nikolayev Vostok-3 (USSR)	94	9	59
14/ 19. 6.63	Lt. Col. V. F. Bykovsky Vostok-5 (USSR)	118	56	41
21/ 29. 8.65	Maj. G. Cooper, Cdr. C. P. Conrad Jr. Gemini GT-5 (USA)	190	55	14.5

		h.	min.	sec.
4/ 18.12.65	Lt. Col. F. Borman, Capt. J. A. Lovell Gemini GT-7 (USA)	330	35	
1/ 19. 6.70	Maj. A. G. Nikolayev, V. I. Sevastyanov Soyuz-9 (USSR)	424	58	55

Feminine Duration

		h.	min.	sec.
16/ 19. 6.63	V. V. Tereshkova Vostok-6 (USSR)	70	40	48

Altitude

		km
12. 4.61	Maj. Y. A. Gagarin Vostok-1 (USSR)	327
12/ 13.10.64	V. M. Komarov, K. P. Feoktistov, B. B. Yegorov Voskhod-1 (USSR)	408
18. 3.65	K. P. Belyayev, Lt. Col. A. A. Leonov Voskhod-2 (USSR)	497.7
12/ 15. 9.66	Cdr. C. P. Conrad Jr., Lt. Col. R. F. Gordon Gemini GT-11 (USA)	1369
21/ 27.12.68	Lt. Col. F. Borman, Capt. J. A. Lovell, W. A. Anders Apollo 8 (USA)	377,668.9

Altitude without earth orbit
(later dropped as World Record)

5. 5.61	Cdr. A. B. Shepard Jr. Mercury Freedom 7 (USA)	187.5

Feminine Altitude

16/ 19. 6.63	V. V. Tereshkova Vostok-6 (USSR)	231.1

Distance

6. 8.61	Maj. G. S. Titov Vostok-2 (USSR)	703,143
11/ 15. 8.62	Maj. A. G. Nikolayev Vostok-3 (USSR)	2,639,600
14/ 19. 6.63	Lt. Col. V. F. Bylovsky Vostok-5 (USSR)	3,325,957
21/ 29. 8.65	Maj. G. Cooper, C. P. Conrad Jr. Gemini GT-5 (USA)	5,331,752
4/ 18.12.65	Lt. Col. F. Borman, Capt. J. A. Lovell Gemini GT-7 (USA)	9,204,575
1/ 19. 6.70	Maj. A. G. Nikolayev, V. I. Sevastyanov Soyuz-9 (USSR)	11,889,027

Feminine Distance

16/ 19. 6.63	V. V. Tereshkova Vostok-6 (USSR)	1,970,990

Greatest Mass Lifted to Altitude

		kg
12. 4.61	Maj. Y. A. Gagarin Vostok-1 (USSR)	4,725
12/ 13.10.64	V. M. Komarov, K. P. Feoktistov, B. B. Yegorov Voskhod-1 (USSR)	5,320
26/ 30.10.68	G. T. Beregovoy Soyuz-3 (USSR)	6,575
21/ 27.12.68	Lt. Col. F. Borman, Capt. J. A. Lovell, W. A. Anders Apollo 8 (USA)	127,980

Greatest Mass Lifted to Altitude without earth orbit

5. 5.61	Cdr. A. B. Shepard Jr Mercury Freedom 7 (USA)	1,832.51

Feminine Greatest Mass Lifted to Altitude

16/ 19. 6.63	V. V. Tereshkova Vostok-6 (USSR)	4,713

Extravehicular duration

		h.	min.	sec.
16. 7.69	N. M. Armstrong Apollo 14 (USA)	2	31	40
19/ 20.11.69	Cdr. C. P. Conrad Jr. Apollo 12 (USA)	7	37	52
5/ 6. 2.71	Cdr. A. B. Shepard Jr. Apollo 14 (USA)	9	12	27
31.7/ 2. 8.71	Col. D. R. Scott Apollo 15 (USA)	18	18	26

Number of Astronauts Remaining simultaneously outside Vehicle

14/ 18. 1.69	A. S. Yeliseyev, Col. Y. V. Khrunov Soyuz-4 and -5 (USSR)	37min

Accumulated Space Flight Time

		days	h.	min.	sec.
4/ 18.12.65	Capt. J. A. Lovell Gemini GT-7	13	18	35	00
11/ 15.11.68	Capt. J. A. Lovell Gemini GT-12	3	22	34	34
21/ 27.12.68	Capt. J. A. Lovell Apollo 8	6	03	00	42
11/ 17. 4.70	Capt. J. A. Lovell Apollo 13	5	19	04	41
	total	29	19	04	57

THE WORLD SPEED RECORD

Date	Pilot, Aircraft, hp/Engine, Locality	Speed in km
12.11.06	Alberto Santos-Dumont 14bis, 50hp Antoinette Bagatelle	41·29
26.10.07	Henri Farman Voisin, 50hp Antoinette Issy-les-Moulineaux	52·700
20. 5.09	Paul Tissandier Wright Flyer, 25/30hp Wright Pont Long, Pau	54·810
23. 8.09	Glenn Curtiss Curtiss, 30hp Curtiss Betheny, Rheims	69·821
24. 8.09	Louis Blériot Blériot XII, 50hp E.N.V. Bétheny, Rheims	74·318
28. 8.09	Louis Blériot Blériot XI, 40hp Anzani Bétheny, Rheims	76·955
23. 4.10	Hubert Latham Antoinette, 50hp Antoinette Nice	77·579
10. 7.10	Léon F. Morane Blériot, 50hp Gnôme Rheims	106·508
3. 9.10	Edouard Nieuport Nieuport, 28hp Nieuport Châlons	108·958
29.10.10	Alfred Leblanc Blériot, 50hp Gnôme New York	109·756
12. 4.11	Alfred Leblanc Blériot, 100hp Gnôme Pau	111·801
11. 5.11	Edouard Nieuport Nieuport, 38hp Nieuport Mourmelon, Châlons	119·760
12. 6.11	Alfred Leblanc Blériot, 100hp Gnôme Etampes	125·000
16. 6.11	Edouard Nieuport Nieuport, 70hp Gnôme Châlons, Mourmelon	130·057
21. 6.11	Edouard Nieuport Nieuport, 70hp Gnôme Mourmelon, Châlons	133·136
13. 1.12	Jules Védrines Deperdussin, 100hp Gnôme Pau	145·161
22. 2.12	Jules Védrines Deperdussin, 130hp Gnôme Pau	161·290
29. 2.12	Jules Védrines Deperdussin, 130hp Gnôme Pau	162·454
1. 3.12	Jules Védrines Deperdussin, 130hp Gnôme Pau	166·821
2. 3.12	Jules Védrines Deperdussin, 130hp Gnôme Pau	167·910
13. 7.12	Jules Védrines Deperdussin, 130hp Gnôme Pau	170·777
9. 9.12	Jules Védrines Deperdussin, 140hp Gnôme Chicago	174·100
8. 6.13	Marcel Prévost Deperdussin, 140hp Gnôme Rheims	179·820
27. 9.13	Marcel Prévost Deperdussin, 160hp Gnôme Rheims	191·897
29. 9.13	Marcel Prévost Deperdussin, 160hp Gnôme Rheims	203·850
7. 2.20	Sadi Lecointe Nieuport 29, 300hp Hispano-Suiza Villacoublay	275·264
8. 2.20	Jean Casale SPAD-Herbemont, 300hp H-S Villacoublay	283·464
9.10.20	Bernard de Romanet SPAD-Herbemont, 300hp H-S Buc	292·682
10.10.20	Sadi Lecointe Nieuport 29, 300hp H-S Buc	296·694
20.10.20	Sadi Lecointe Nieuport 29, 300hp H-S Villacoublay	302·529
4.11.20	Bernard de Romanet SPAD-Herbemont, 300hp H-S Buc	309·012
12.12.20	Sadi Lecointe Nieuport 29, 300hp H-S Buc	313·043
26. 9.21	Sadi Lecointe Nieuport-Delage, 300hp H-S Villesauvage-la-Marmogne	330·275
21. 9.22	Sadi Lecointe Nieuport-Delage, 300hp H-S Villesauvage	341·023
13.10.22	Brig.-Gen. W. Mitchell Curtiss Racer, 375hp Curtiss D-12 Detroit	358·836

Date	Pilot, Aircraft, hp/Engine, Locality	Speed in km
15. 2.23	Sadi Lecointe / Nieuport-Delage, 400hp H-S / Istres	375·000
29. 3.23	Lt. R. L. Maughan / Curtiss R-6, 465hp Curtiss / Wright Field, Ohio	380·751
2.11.23	Lt. H. J. Brown, USN / Curtiss Navy Racer, 600hp Curtiss / Mineola	417·059
4.11.23	Lt. A. J. Williams, USN / Curtiss Navy Racer, 600hp Curtiss / Mineola	429·025
11.12.24	Adj. A. Bonnet / SIMB Bernard-Ferbois V-2, 550hp H-S / Istres	448·171
14.11.27	Cdt. Mario de Bernardi / Macchi M.52, 1000hp FIAT A.S.3 / Venice Lido (Class C bis) Class C bis is the FAI record class for seaplanes	473·820
30. 3.28	Cdt. Mario de Bernardi / Macchi M.52, 1000hp FIAT A.S.3 / Venice Lido (Class C bis).	512·776
10. 9.29	F/O. G. H. Stainforth / Gloster VI, 1400hp Napier Lion VIID / Calshot (Class C bis)	541·100
12. 9.29	S/Ldr. A. H. Orlebar / Supermarine S.6, 1900hp Rolls-Royce R / Calshot (Class C bis)	575·700
29. 9.31	Ft.-Lt. G. H. Stainforth / Supermarine S.6B, 2600hp Rolls-Royce R / Lee-on-Solent (Class C bis)	655·000
10. 4.33	Lt. Francesco Agello / Macchi-Castoldi M.C.72, 2800hp FIAT-Zerbi A.S.6 / Desenzano (Class C bis)	682·078
23.10.34	Lt. Francesco Agello / Macchi-Castoldi M.C.72, 2800hp FIAT-Zerbi A.S.6 / Desenzano (Class C bis)	709·209
30. 3.39	Fl.Kap.Ing Hans Dieterle / Heinkel He 112U (He 100V8), 1175/1800hp Daimler-Benz DB 601 / Orianenberg	746·604
26. 4.39	Fl.Kap. Fritz Wendel / Messerschmitt Bf 109R (Me 209V1), 1000/2300hp Daimler-Benz DB 601R / Augsburg	755·138
7.11.45	G/Capt. H. J. Wilson / Gloster Meteor IV, 2 × 4000lb Rolls-Royce Derwent V / Herne Bay	975·875
7. 9.46	G/Capt. E. M. Donaldson / Gloster Meteor IV, 2 × 4000lb Rolls-Royce Derwent V / Littlehampton	991·000
19. 6.47	Col. A. Boyd, USAAF / Lockheed P-80R, 5400lb Allison J33 A23 / Muroc, Cal.	1003·811
20. 8.47	Cdr. T. F. Caldwell, USN / Douglas D-558 Skystreak, 3990lb TG180 / Muroc, Cal.	1031·178
25. 8.47	Maj. Marion E. Carl, USMC / Douglas D-558 Skystreak, 3990lb TG180 / Muroc, Cal.	1047·536
15. 9.48	Maj. R. L. Johnson, USAF / North American F-86 A-1 Sabre, 6000lb General Electric J47, GE-1 / Muroc, Cal.	1079·841
19.11.52	Capt. James S. Nash / North American F-86D-5 Sabre, 7630lb General Electric J47-17 / Salton Sea, Cal.	1124·137
16. 7.53	Lt.-Col. William J. Barnes, USAF / North American F-86D-30 Sabre, 7630lb General Electric J47-17 / Salton Sea, Cal.	1151·883
7. 9.53	S/Ldr. Neville F. Duke / Hawker Hunter F1, Rolls-Royce Avon RA 7 / Angmering-Littlehampton	1171·000
25. 9.53	Lt.Cdr. M. J. Lithgow / Supermarine Swift F 4, Rolls-Royce Avon / Azizia, Tripoli	1184·000
3.10.53	Lt.-Cdr. James B. Verdin, USN / Douglas XF4D, Westinghouse J40-WE-8 / Salton Sea, Cal.	1211·746
29.10.53	Lt.-Col. Frank K. Everest, Jr., USAF / North American YF-100A, 9700lb Pratt and Whitney J57-P7 / Salton Sea, Cal.	1215·298
20. 8.55	Col. H. A. Hanes, USAF / North American YF-100C, 11,700lb Pratt and Whitney J57-P21 / Palmdale-Mint Canyon, Cal.	1323·312
10. 3.56	L. Peter Twiss / Fairey FD 2, 10,000lb Rolls-Royce Avon Srs. 200 / Ford-Chichester	1822·000
12.12.57	Maj. Adrian E. Drew, USAF / McDonnell F-101A Voodoo, 2 × 15,000lb Pratt and Whitney J57-P13 / Edwards AFB	1943·500
16. 5.58	Capt. Walter W. Irwin, USAF / Lockheed F-104A Starfighter, General Electric J79-GE3 / Edwards AFB	2259·538
31.10.59	Gueorgui Mossolov / E-66, 13,000lb TRD RS7F / Joukovski–Petrovskoe	2388·000
15.12.59	Maj. Joseph W. Rogers, USAF / Convair F-106A, 24,500lb Pratt and Whitney J75-P17 / Edwards AFB	2455·736
22.11.61	Lt.-Col. Robert B. Robinson, USMC / McDonnell F4H-1F, 2 × 20,000/31,000lb General Electric J79-8GE / Edwards AFB	2585·425
7. 7.62	Lt.-Col. Georgi Mossolov / Mikoyan E-166, 22,046lb TRD P.166 / Podmoskovnöe	2681·000
1. 5.65	Col. R. Stevens, USAF / Lockheed YF-12A, 2 × 30,000lb Pratt and Whitney JT-11B-20D / Edwards AFB	3731·507

THE WORLD DISTANCE RECORD

Date	Pilot, Aircraft, hp/Engine, Locality	km
12.11.06	A. Santos-Dumont / 14 bis, 50hp Antoinette / Bagatelle	0·220
26.10.07	Henri Farman / Voisin, 50hp Antoinette / Issy-les-Moulineaux	0·770
13. 1.08	Henri Farman / Voisin, 50hp Antoinette / Issy	1·000
21. 3.08	Henri Farman / Voisin, 50hp Antoinette / Issy	2·004
11. 4.08	Léon Delagrange / Voisin, 50hp Antoinette / Issy	3·925
30. 5.08	Léon Delagrange / Voisin, 50hp Antoinette / Cantocelle	12·75
6. 9.08	Léon Delagrange / Voisin, 50hp Antoinette / Issy	24·125
21. 9.08	Wilbur Wright / Wright flyer, 22/25hp Wright / Auvours Camp, le Mans	66·6
18.12.08	Wilbur Wright / Wright flyer, 22/25hp Wright / Auvours	93·8
31.12.08	Wilbur Wright / Wright flyer, 22/25hp Wright / Auvours	124·7
25. 8.09	Louis Paulhan / Voisin, 50hp Gnôme / Bétheny, Rheims	134·000
26. 8.09	Hubert Latham / Antoinette, 50hp Antoinette / Bétheny	154·620
27. 8.09	Henri Farman / Farman, 50hp Gnôme / Bétheny	180·000
4.11.09	Henri Farman / Farman, 50hp Gnôme / Mourmelon, Châlons	234·212
9. 7.10	René Labouchère / Antoinette, 50hp Antoinette / Rheims	340·000
10. 7.10	Jan Olieslagers / Blériot, 60hp Gnôme / Rheims	392·750
28.10.10	Maurice Tabuteau / Maurice Farman, 50/60hp Renault / Etampes	465·720
21.12.10	Georges Legagneux / Blériot, 50hp Gnôme / Pau	515·900
30.12.10	Maurice Tabuteau / Maurice Farman, 50/60hp Renault / Buc	584·745
16. 7.11	Jan Olieslagers / Blériot, 50hp Gnôme / Kiewit-les-Hasselt	625·000
1. 9.11	Fourny / Maurice Farman, 50/60hp Renault / Buc	722·935
24.12.11	Armand Gobé / Nieuport, 50hp Gnôme / Pau	740·299
11. 9.12	Fourny / Maurice Farman, 50/60hp Renault / Etampes	1010·900

In August, 1913, distance flights in a straight line were admitted for world record classification, although balloon records were not listed as such by the FAI at the time. The list of straight line distance records given below may, by the help of the dates, be tied in with the closed circuit list to see in which category, after 1913, lay the record distance of the period. The balloon records are of considerable interest in themselves, in view of the distance traversed and the ease with which, in those days, frontiers could be crossed.

Date	Pilot, Aircraft, hp/Engine, Locality	km

Distance in a Straight Line

Date	Pilot, Aircraft, hp/Engine, Locality	km
9/11 .10.1900	Count de la Vaulx / Vincennes–Korostychey (Russia)	1925·000
7/ 8. 1.12	Emile Dubonnet and Dupont / "Condor III" / Lamotte Breuil–Sokolowska (Russia)	1953·898
27/ 29.10.12	M. Bienaimé / Stuttgart–Riazan (Russia)	2191·000
19/ 21. 3.13	R. Rumpelmayer / Lamotte Breuil–Voltsthyvar (Russia)	2420·653
13/ 17.12.13	Hugo Kaulen, Schmitz, Krest / "Duisburg" / Bitterfeld–St. Petersburg/Perm (Russia)	2827·900
8/ 10. 2.14	Berliner / Bitterfeld–Bissertsk (Russia)	3052·700
3/ 4. 2.25	Capts. Arrachart and Lemaître / Bréguet XIX B-2, 480hp Renault / Etampes–Villa Cisneros	3166·300
28/ 29.10.26	Dieudonné Costes and Rignot / Bréguet XIX, 500hp Hispano / Le Bouget–Jask (Persia)	5396·000
4/ 6. 6.27	Clarence D. Chamberlain and Charles A. Levine / Bellanca "Miss Columbia", 200hp Wright J-5 / Roosevelt Field–Helfa (Germany)	6294·000
3/ 5. 6.28	Capt. Arturo Ferrarin, Major Carlo P. de Preto / Savoia-Marchetti S-65, 550hp FIAT A22 / Montecelio–Touros (Brazil)	7188·260
27/ 29. 9.29	Dieudonné Costes, Maurice Bellonte / Bréguet XIX "Point d'Interrogation," 600hp H-S / Le Bourget–Moulart (China)	7905·140
28/ 30. 7.31	Russel N. Boardman, John Polando / Bellanca "Cape Cod," 300hp Wright J-6 / Brooklyn–Istambul	8065·736
6/ 8. 2.33	S/Ldr. O. R. Gayford, Flt.-Lt. G. E. Nicholetts / Fairey long range, 600hp Napier Lion / Cranwell–Walvis Bay	8544·000
5/ 7. 8.33	Paul Codos, Maurice Rossi / Blériot-Zapata 110, "Joseph le Brix," 550hp Hispano-Suiza / Floyd Bennett–Rayack (Syria)	9104·700
5/ 7. 8.33	Paul Codos, Maurice Rossi / Blériot-Zapata 110 "Joseph le Brix," 550hp Hispano-Suiza / Floyd Bennett–Le Bouget–Rhodes–Rayack / (Distance in a broken line)	9106·330
12/ 14. 7.37	Col. M. Gromov, Cdr. A. Youmachev, Eng. S. Daniline / ANT 25-1, 860hp AM-34 / Moscow/Tchelkovo–San Jacinto, Cal.	10,148·000
1.10.46	Cdr. Thomas D. Davies, Cdr. Eugene P. Rankin, Cdr. W. S. Reid, Lt.-Cdr. Ray A. Tabeling, USN / Lockheed P2V-1 Neptune "Truculent Turtle," 2 × 2300lb Wright R-3350-8A / Pierce Field, Perth–Port Columbus, Ohio	18,081·990
10/ 11. 1.62	Maj. Clyde P. Eveley, USAF / Boeing B-52H, 8 × 17,000lb Pratt and Whitney TF-33-P-3 / Okinawa–Madrid	20,168·780

Distance in Closed Circuit

Date	Pilot, Aircraft, hp/Engine, Locality	km
3/ 4. 6.20	Lucien Bossoutrot and Jean Bernard / Farman Goliath, 2 × 260hp Salmson / Villesauvage-la-Marmogne	1915·200
16/ 17. 4.23	Lt. Oakley J. Kelly and Lt. John McReady / Fokker T-2, 400 Liberty	4050·000
7/ 9. 8.25	Drouhin and Landry / Farman, 450hp Farman / Etampes	4400·000
3/ 5. 8.27	Edzard and Ristics / Junkers W.33, 230hp Junkers L-5 / Dessau	4660·628
31. 5.28 to 2. 6.28	Capt. Arturo Ferrarin and Major P. de Prete / Savoia-Marchetti S 64, 550hp FIAT A22 / Rome	7666·616
15/ 17.12.29	Dieudonné Costes and Paul Codos / Breguet XIX, 600hp Hispano-Suiza / Istres	8029·440
30. 5.30 to 2. 6.30	Umberto Maddalena and Fausto Cecconi / Savoia-Marchetti S.64 bis, 550hp FIAT A22T / Montecelio	8188·800

Date	Pilot, Aircraft, hp/Engine, Locality	km
26. 2.31 to 1. 3.31	Lucien Bossoutrot and Capt. Maurice Rossi / Blériot-Zapata 110, 600hp Hispano-Suiza / Oran	8822·315
7/ 10. 6.31	Joseph le Brix and Marcel Doret / Dewoitine "Arc-en-Ciel," 650hp Hispano-Suiza / Istres	10,372·051
23/ 26. 3.32	Lucien Bossoutrot and Capt. Maurice Rossi / Blériot-Zapata 110, 600hp Hispano-Suiza	10,601·480
13/ 15. 5.38	Cotyûzô Fujito, Sgt. Major Takahshi, mech. Sekine / Koken long range monoplane, 700hp Kawasaki	11,651·011
30. 7.39 to 1. 8.39	Lt.-Col. Angelo Tondi, Capt. Roberto Dagasso, Mar. Ferrugio Vignoli, Aldo Stagnali / Savoia-Marchetti SM-82D, 3 ×860hp Alfa-Romeo 128 RC-21 / Rome	12,935·770
1/ 3. 8.47	Lt.-Col. Owen F. Lassiter, USAF / Boeing B-29, 4 × 2200hp Wright / Tampa, Florida	14,249·656
14.12.60	Lt.-Col. Thomas W. Grissom, USAF / Boeing B-52G, 8 × 9500lb Pratt and Whitney P-43 / Edwards AFB	16,220·360
6/ 7. 6.62	Capt. William B. Stevenson, USAF / Boeing B-52H, 8 × 17,000lb Pratt ard Whitney TF-33-P-3 / Seymour AFB	18,245·050

THE ALTITUDE RECORD

As in the case of other world records, progress was, in the early days, measured by standards of aeroplanes only – Class C. But it is a suitable reminder of the slow and painful progress away from the ground of the heavier-than-air machine to note, before beginning the long list of altitude records, the actual best performance in any Class at the start of the century.

Date	Pilot, Aircraft, hp/Engine, Locality	m
31. 7.01	Suring and Berson / balloon / Berlin / This was not beaten by an aeroplane until 1923.	10,800
29. 8.09	Hubert Latham / Antoinette, 50hp Antoinette / Rheims	155
18.10.09	Comte de Lambert / Wright, 22/25hp Barriquand & Marré / Paris	300
1.12.09	Hubert Latham / Antoinette, 50hp Antoinette / Châlons	453
7. 1.10	Hubert Latham / Antoinette, 50hp Antoinette / Châlons	1,000
12. 1.10	Louis Paulhan / Henri Farman, 50hp Gnôme / Los Angeles	1,209
14. 6.10	Walter Brookins / Wright, 30hp Wright / Indianapolis	1,335
7. 7.10	Hubert Latham / Antoinette, 50hp Antoinette / Rheims	1,384
10. 7.10	Walter Brookins / Wright, 30hp Wright / Atlantic City	1,900
11. 8.10	J. Armstrong Drexel / Blériot, 50hp Gnôme / Lanark	2,012
3. 9.10	Léon F. Morane / Blériot, 50hp Gnôme / Deauville	2,582
8. 9.10	Géo. Chavez / Blériot, 50hp Gnôme / Issy-les-Moulineaux	2,587
1.10.10	Henri Wynmalen / Henri Farman, 50hp Gnôme / Châlons	2,780
—.10.10	J. Armstrong Drexel / Blériot, 50hp Gnôme / Philadelphia	2,880
31.10.10	Ralph Johnston / Baby Wright, 30hp Wright / Belmont Park	2,960
8.12.10	Georges Legagneux / Blériot, 50hp Gnôme / Pau	3,100
8. 7.11	Marcel Loridan / Henri Farman racer, 50hp Gnôme / Châlons	3,177
9. 8.11	Capt. Julien Félix / Blériot, 50 or 70hp Gnôme / Etampes	3,190
4. 9.11	Roland Garros / Blériot, 50/70hp Gnôme / Parame, nr. St. Malo	3,910
6. 9.12	Roland Garros / Blériot special, 50/70hp Gnôme / Houlgate	4,900
7. 9.12	Georges Legagneux / Morane-Borel, 50/70hp Gnôme / Corbaulieu	5,450
11.12.12	Roland Garros / Morane-Saulnier, 50/70hp Gnôme / Tunis	5,610
11. 3.13	Edmond Perreyon / Blériot, 70hp Gnôme / Buc	5,880
28.12.13	Georges Legagneux / Nieuport, 80hp Rhône / St. Raphaël	6,120
27. 2.20	Maj. Rudolf W. Schroeder / LePère, 400hp Liberty / Dayton, Ohio	10,093
18. 9.21	Lt. John MacReady / LePère, 400hp Liberty / Dayton, Ohio	10,518
5. 9.23	Sadi Lecointe / Nieuport-Delage, 300hp H-S / Villacoublay	10,741
30.10.23	Sadi Lecointe / Nieuport-Delage, 300hp H-S / Issy-les-Moulineaux	11,415
10.10.24	Callizo / Gordou-Leseure, 300hp H-S s/c / Villacoublay	12,066
23. 8.26	Callizo / Blériot-SPAD, 450hp Lorraine s/c / Buc	12,442
26. 5.29	Willi Neuenhofen / Junkers W.34, 420hp Bristol Jupiter / Dessau	12,739
4. 6.30	Lt. Apollo Soucek / Wright Apache, 450hp Pratt and Whitney Wasp / Washington	13,157
27. 5.31	Prof. Auguste Piccard, Paul Kipfer / balloon	15,781
18. 8.32	Prof. Auguste Piccard, Max Cosyns / balloon	16,201
22.11.33	Lt.-Cdr. T. G. W. Settle, Maj. Chester L. Fordner / balloon / Akron, Ohio	18,665
11.11.35	Capt. Orville A. Anderson, Capt. Albert W. Stevens / balloon "Explorer II" / Rapid City, S. Dakota	22,066
19/ 20. 8.57	Major David G. Simons, USAF / Winzen research balloon / Corsby, Minnesota	30,942
14.12.59	Capt. Joe B. Jordan, USAF / Lockheed F-104C, 15,000lb General Electric J79-GE-7 / Edwards AFB	31,513
28. 4.61	Georgii Mossolov / E-66A 13,200lb TRD, 7600lb GRD / Podmoskovnoie	34,714
30. 4.62	Joseph A. Walker / North American X-15-1, 59,000lb LR-99 / Edwards AFB	75,209
17. 7.62	Maj. Robert M. White / North American X-15-3, 57,000lb LR-99 / Edwards AFB (air-launched)	95,936
23. 4.48	G/Capt. John Cunningham, D.S.O., D.F.C. / D.H. Vampire Mk. 1, 4290lb D.H. Ghost 2/2 / Hatfield	18,119
4. 5.53	Walter Frame Gibb / English Electric Canberra B.2, 2 × 9750lb Bristol Olympus / Filton	19,406
29. 8.55	Walter Frame Gibb / English Electric Canberra B.2, 2 × Bristol Olympus 102 / Filton	20,083
29. 8.57	Michael Randrup and Walter Shirley / English Electric Canberra B.2, 2 × Rolls-Royce Avon, and Napier Double Scorpion rocket / Luton	21,430
18. 4.58	Lt.-Cdr. George C. Watkins, USN / Grumman F-11-1F, 15,000lb General Electric J79-GE-3A / Edwards AFB, Cal.	23,449
2. 5.58	Roger Carpentier / So9050/06 Trident, 2 × 3300lb SEPR-631 rockets, 2 × 2420lb Turboméca / Istres	24,217
7. 5.58	Maj. Howard C. Johnson, USAF / Lockheed F-104A, 15,000lb General Electric J79-GE-7 / Palmdale, Cal.	27,811
14. 7.59	Vladimir Ilyushin / T.431, 19,800lb Mk. 31 / Podmoskovnoie	28,852
6.12.59	Cdr. Lawrence D. Flint, USN / McDonnell F4H-1, 15,000lb General Electric J79-GE-2 / Edwards AFB	30,042

The Class C and World record lines merge again after this last record, with that of Captain Jordan on 14.12.59.

Between the years 1931 and 1957, the record was firmly in the hands of Class A, spherical balloons. The Class C International records for aeroplanes during this period, although not world records, are given below in order to complete the story of the development of this record in the hands of heavier-than-air craft.

Class C International Records, 1932-59

Date	Pilot, Aircraft, hp/Engine, Locality	m
16. 9.32	Capt. Cyril Frank Uwins / Vickers Vespa, Bristol Pegasus S.3 / Filton	13,404
28. 9.33	Lemoine / Potez 506, Gnôme-Rhône 14 Kbrs / Villacoublay	13,661
11. 4.34	Cdt. Renato Donati / Caproni, 600hp Bristol Pegasus / Rome	14,443
14. 8.36	Georges Détré / Potez 506, Gnôme-Rhône 14 Krsd / Villacoublay	14,843
28. 9.36	S/Ldr. F. R. D. Swain / Bristol 138, 490hp Bristol Pegasus PE VI S / South Farnborough	15,223
8. 5.37	Mario Pezzi / Caproni 161 bis, Piaggio XI-R.C.72 / Montecelio	15,655
30. 6.37	Flt.-Lt. M. J. Adam / Bristol 138A, 490hp Bristol Pegasus / South Farnborough	16,440
22.10.38	Lt.-Col. Mario Pezzi / Caproni Ca 161 bis, Piaggio XI-R.C.72 / Montecelio	17,083

THE SCHNEIDER TROPHY

Aircraft (Engine), Pilot	Speed	Place
16.4.13 Monaco 28 x 10km laps = 280km = 150nm 172·83sm		
France		
Bréguet (200 Salmson/Canton-Unné) / René Moineau	—	Eliminated
Bréguet (110/115 Salmson/Canton-Unné) / Henri Brégi	—	Eliminated
Nieuport (50 Gnôme) / Dr. Gabriel Espanet	—	Retired lap 8
Nieuport (100 Gnôme) / —	—	Eliminated
Deperdussin (160 Gnôme) / Maurice Prévost	45·75	1st
Deperdussin (160 Gnôme) / —	—	Eliminated
Borel Monaco (160 Gnôme) / Géo. Chemet	—	Eliminated
Morane-Saulnier (80 Gnôme) / Roland Garros	30·42	At 3rd attempt
USA		
Nieuport (160 Gnôme) / Charles T. Weymann	—	Retired lap 25
20.4.14 Monaco 28 x 10km = 280km = 150nm = 172·83sm		
UK		
Morane-Saulnier (80 Gnôme) / Lord Carbery	—	Crashed on trial
Sopwith Schneider (100 Mono Gnôme) / C. Howard Pixton	86·78	1st
France		
Nieuport (160 Gnôme) / Dr. Gabriel Espanet	—	Retired lap 16
Nieuport (160 Gnôme) / Pierre Levasseur	—	Retired lap 17
Morane-Saulnier (160 Gnôme) / Roland Garros	Prop broke on t/o	
Deperdussin (160 Gnôme) / Maurice Prévost	—	Withdrew
Morane-Saulnier (160 Gnôme) / Marcel Brindejonc des Moulinais	—	2nd reserve
Deperdussin (160 Gnôme) / L. Janoir	—	3rd reserve
USA		
Nieuport (160 le Rhône) / Charles T. Weymann	—	Withdrew
Deperdussin (160 Gnôme) / William Thaw	—	Withdrew
Lawrence Sperry	—	1st reserve
Lincoln Beachy	—	2nd reserve
Germany		
Aviatik (100 Benz) / Victor Stoeffler	—	Crashed on trials

Aircraft (Engine), Pilot	Speed	Place

Switzerland
FBA (100 Mono Gnôme)
  Ernest Burri — **51·00** **2nd**
Deperdussin (160 Gnôme)
  Parmelin — **Reserve**

10.9.19 Bournemouth 10 x 20nm = 200nm = 230·3sm = 370.6km

UK
Fairey III (450 Napier Lion)
  Lt.-Col. Vincent Nicholl, D.S.O., D.S.C. — **Retired – fog**
Sopwith Schneider (450 Cosmos Jupiter)
  H. G. Hawker, O.B.E., A.F.C. — **Damaged on trials**
Supermarine Sea Lion I (450 Napier Lion II)
  S/Ldr. Basil D. Hobbs, D.S.O., D.F.C. — **Damaged on trials**
Avro 539A Schneider (240 Siddeley Puma)
  Capt. H. A. Hamersley, M.C. — **Reserve; damaged**

France
Nieuport 29C-1 (300 Hispano-Suiza)
  Lt. Jean Casale — **Damaged at Cowes**
Nieuport 29C-1 (300 Hispano-Suiza)
  Malard — **Did not arrive**
S.P.A.D.-Herbémont 20 (300 Hispano-Suiza)
  Sadi Lecointe — **Damaged**

Italy
S.I.A.I. Savoia S.13 (250 Isotta-Fraschini)
  Serg. Guido Janello — **109·77**

21.9.20 Venice 10 x 37·5 km = 375km = 202·2nm = 233sm

Italy
S.I.A.I. Savoia S.19 (470/550 Ansaldo St. Giorgio 4E-284)
  Lt. Luigi Bologna — **107·22** **1st**
S.I.A.I. Savoia S.19 (470/550 Ansaldo St. Giorgio 4E-284)
  Serg. Guido Janello — **Withdrew**
Nieuport-Macchi M-XIX (470/550 Ansaldo St. Giorgio 4E-284)
  Arturo Zanetti — **Withdrew**
Nieuport-Macchi M-XII (680 F.I.A.T. A-14)
  Giovanni de Briganti — **Withdrew**

France
S.P.A.D. — **Wrecked on early tests**
Nieuport —

7.8.21 Venice 10 x 37·06km = 370·6km = 230·3sm = 200nm

Italy
Macchi M-VII (200 Isotta-Fraschini)
  Giovanni de Briganti — **110·9** **1st**
Macchi Naval (250 Isotta-Fraschini)
  Piero Corgnilio — **Ran out of fuel**
Macchi M-XIX (700 F.I.A.T.)
  Arturo Zanetti — **Caught fire**

France
Nieuport-Delage (300 Hispano-Suiza)
  Sadi Lecointe — **Crashed on test**

12.8.22 Naples 13 x 28·5km = 370·5km = 200nm = 230·3sm

UK
Supermarine Sea Lion II (450 Napier Lion)
  Capt. H. C. Biard — **145·7** **1st**

Italy
Macchi M-VII (200 Isotta-Fraschini)
  Alessandro Passaleva — **2nd**
Macchi Naval (250 Isotta-Fraschini)
  Piero Corniglio — **4th**
S.I.A.I. Savoia S.19 (450/500 Ansaldo)
  Arturo Zanetti — **3rd**

France
C.A.M.S. 31 (300 Hispano-Suiza)
  V. Roman — **Not ready**
C.A.M.S. 31 (300 Hispano-Suiza)
  Capit. de Corv. Teste — **Not ready**

28.9.23 Cowes 5 x 37·2nm = 186nm = 214·7sm = 344·69km

USA
Curtiss CR-3 (465/500 Curtiss D-12A)
  Lt. Rutledge Irving, USN — **173·46** **2nd**
Curtiss CR-3 (465/500 Curtiss D-12A)
  Lt. David Rittenhouse, USN — **177·38** **1st**
Curtis TR-3A (290/300 Wright E-4)
  Lt. Frank W. Wead, USN — **Non-starter**
Wright N.W.2. (575/650 Wright T-3)
  Lt. A. W. Gorton, U.S.N. — **Sank on trials**

UK
Supermarine Sea Lion III (550 Napier Lion)
  Capt. H. C. Biard — **151·56** **3rd**

Blackburn Pellet (450 Napier Lion)
  L/Cdr. R. W. Kenworthy — **Sank on trials**
Hawker-Sopwith (400 Bristol-Cosmos Jupiter)
  F/Lt. Longton — **Damaged en route**

France
C.A.M.S. 38 (360 Hispano-Suiza)
  Lt. de V. Maurice Hurel — **Retired lap 2**
C.A.M.S. 36bis (300 Hispano-Suiza)
  Pelletier d'Oisy — **Damaged – withdrawn**
S.I.C.C. Latham L.1 (2x 400 Lorraine-Dietrich)
  Duhamel — **Withdrawn**
S.I.C.C. Latham L.1 (2x 400 Lorraine-Dietrich)
  — **Damaged – withdrawn**

25.10.24 Baltimore 7 x 27nm = 189nm = 217·6sm = 350.37km

UK
Gloster-Napier II (630 Napier Lion)
  Capt. Hubert S. Broad — **Sank on test**
Supermarine (Rolls-Royce Condor) — **Not completed**

Italy
Piaggio (300 Hispano-Suiza) — **Withdrawn**
Macchi — **Withdrawn**
Montfalcone — **Withdrawn**

USA
Curtiss CR-3 (465/500 Crutiss D-12A)
Curtiss CR-3 (465/500 Curtiss D-12A)
Curtiss R2C-2 (465/500 Curtiss D-12A)
Curtiss R2C-2 (465/500 Curtiss D-12A)
Wright F-2W
  Lts. Rittenhouse, Wead, Gorton from previous team; Lt. G. T. Cuddihy, Lt. R. A. Ofstie, Lt. L. D. Hunt, Boatswain E. E. Reber, reserves
Following withdrawal of all foreign entries, USA very sportingly withdrew her team, postponing contest for one year and forfeiting her chance to win the Cup outright with a "fly-over".

26.10.25 Chesapeake Bay 7 x 27nm = 189nm = 217·6sm = 350·37km

USA
Curtiss R3C-2 (600 Curtiss V-1400)
  Lt. George T. Cuddihy, USN — **Retired last lap**
Curtiss R3C-2 (600 Curtiss V-1400)
  Lt. Ralph A. Ofstie, USN — **Retired lap 6**
Curtiss R3C-2 (600 Curtiss V-1400)
  Lt. James H. Doolittle, USAAS — **232·573** **1st**

UK
Supermarine-Napier S-4 (700 Napier Lion VII)
  Capt. H. C. Biard — **Crashed on trials**
Gloster-Napier III (700 Napier Lion VII)
  Capt. Hubert S. Broad — **199·169** **2nd**
Gloster-Napier III (700 Napier Lion VII)
  S/Ldr. H. J. L. Hinkler — **Failed on trials**

Italy
Macchi M-33 (465/500 Curtiss D-12A)
  Giovanni de Briganti — **168·44** **3rd***
Macchi M-33 (465/500 Curtiss D-12A)
  Lt. Morselli — **Withdrew**
*Mistook turning point and did 4 extra miles per lap, hence low speed.

13.11.26 Hampton Roads 7 x 27nm = 189nm = 217·6sm = 350·37km

Italy
Macchi-F.I.A.T. M-39 (800/880 F.I.A.T. A.S.2)
  Magg. Mario de Bernardi — **246·496** **1st**
Macchi-F.I.A.T. M-39 (800/880 F.I.A.T. A.S.2)
  Capit. Arturo Ferrarin — **Retired lap 4**
Macchi-F.I.A.T. M-39 (800/882 F.I.A.T. A.S.2)
  Ten. Adriano Bacula — **218·006** **3rd**

USA
Curtiss R3C-4 (700 Curtiss V-1550)
  Lt. George T. Cuddihy — **Retired lap 7**
Curtiss R3C-2 (600 Curtiss V-1400)
  Lt. Christian F. Schilt, USN — **231·363** **2nd**
Curtiss-Packard R3C-2 (700 Packard V-1500)
  Lt. William Tomlinson, USN — **Crashed on trials**
Curtiss F6C-1 Hawk (500 Curtiss D-12A)
  Lt. William Tomlinson — **136·953** **Reserve a/c 4th**

UK
Supermarine-Napier S-5 } Delayed, waiting for mock-up of
Gloster-Napier IV } new Lion.

26.9.27 Venice Lido 7 x 50km = 350km = 188·8nm = 217·4sm

UK
Short Crusader (800 Bristol Mercury)
  F/Lt. H. M. Schofield — **Crashed 11.9.27**

Supermarine-Napier S.5/25 (875 geared Napier Lion VIIB)
  F/Lt. S. N. Webster, A.F.C. — **281·656** **1st**
Supermarine-Napier S.5/21 (875 Napier Lion VIIB)
  F/Lt. O. E. Worsley — **272·91** **2nd**
Gloster-Napier IVB (875 geared Napier Lion VIIB)
  F/Lt. S. M. Kinkhead, D.S.O., D.S.C., D.F.C. — **Retired lap 6**
Gloster-Napier IV (700 Napier Lion VII) — **Reserve**
Gloster-Napier IVA (700 Napier Lion VII) — **Reserve**

Italy
Macchi-F.I.A.T. M-52 (1000 F.I.A.T. A.S.3)
  Col. Mario de Bernardi — **Retired lap 2**
Macchi-F.I.A.T. M-52 (1000 F.I.A.T. A.S.3)
  Comm. Arturo Ferrarin — **Retired lap 1**
Macchi-F.I.A.T. M-52 (1000 F.I.A.T. A.S.3)
  Capit. Federico Guazzetti — **Retired lap 7**
Macchi-F.I.A.T. M-52 (880 F.I.A.T. A.S.2)
  Capit. Guascone Guasconi — **Reserve**

USA
Packard-Kirkham (1200 Packard X-2750)
  Maj. Alford J. Williams — **Not ready**

7.9.29 Solent 7 x 50km = 350km = 188·8nm = 217·4sm

UK
Gloster-Napier VI (1400 s/c Napier Lion VIID)
  S/Ldr. A. H. Orlebar, AFC — **Withdrawn**
Gloster-Napier VI (1400 s/c Napier Lion VIID)
  F/Lt. G. H. Stainforth — **Withdrawn**
Supermarine R-R S.6 (1900 Rolls-Royce 'R')
  F/Lt. H. R. D. Waghorn — **328·63** **1st**
Supermarine R-R S.6 (1900 Rolls-Royce 'R')
  F/O R. L. R. Atcherley — **325·54** **Disqualified**
Supermarine-Napier S.5 (875 Napier Lion VIIB)
  F/Lt. D. D'Arcy A. Greig, D.F.C., A.F.C. — **282·11** **3rd**

Italy
Macchi-Castoldi M-67 (1500 Isotta-Fraschini)
  Ten. Remo Cadringher — **Retired lap 2**
Macchi-Castoldi M-67 (1500 Isotta-Fraschini)
  Ten. Giovanni Monti — **Retired**
F.I.A.T. C-29 (1000 F.I.A.T.)
  Mar. Francesco Agello — **Withdrawn**
Savoia-Marchetti S-65 (2 x Isotta or F.I.A.T.)
  — **Withdrawn**

Macchi-F.I.A.T. M-52bis (1000 F.I.A.T. A.S.3)
  Mar. Thomaso Dal Molin — **284·2** **2nd**
Macchi-F.I.A.T. M-52 } Reserve aircraft, with long-span
Macchi-F.I.A.T. M-52 } wings and smaller engines
Piaggio P.7 (Isotta-Fraschini) 2 aircraft; not produced for contest.

USA
Packard-Mercury "Hispeed" (1200 Packard X-2750)
  Maj. Alford J. Williams — **Non-arrival**

France
Nieuport (Hispano-Suiza)
Nieuport (Hispano-Suiza)
S.I.M.B. Bernard-Ferbois (Hispano-Suiza)
S.I.M.B. Bernard-Ferbois (Hispano-Suiza) — **Not ready**

13.9.31 Solent 7 x 50km = 350km = 188·8nm = 217·4sm

UK
Supermarine R-R S.6B (2300 Rolls-Royce 'R')
  F/Lt. J. N. Boothman — **340·08** **1st**
Supermarine R-R S.6B (2300 Rolls-Royce 'R')
  F/Lt. F. W. Long — **Reserve 1**
Supermarine R-R S.6A (1900 Rolls-Royce 'R')
  F/O L. S. Snaith — **Reserve 2**
Supermarine R-R S.6A (1900 Rolls-Royce 'R') — **Crashed 9.31.**

France
Nieuport-Delage (Hispano-Suiza)
S.I.M.B. Bernard-Ferbois (Hispano-Suiza)
Dewoitine
  Sadi Lecointe, Jean Assolant, Capt. Vernold (team); Lt. Retourna, Sgt./Maj. Dumas, Sgt. Ballet (reserves).

Italy
Magg. Guglielmo, Casselini, Ten. Pietro Scapellini, Ten. Stanislao Bellini, Ten. Ariosto Neri, Mar. Francesco Agello.
Neither Italy nor France could produce a team in time and had no valid grounds for a postponement of the contest. No challenger having appeared within the next five years, the Trophy became the absolute property of the Royal Aero Club.